The Entrepreneurial

Airbnb Hosting Guide

Super Host Your Way to Personal and Financial Freedom and Grow Your Wealth with Insider Step by Step Guide to Create A Million Dollar Airbnb Business

Table Of Contents

Introduction

Airbnb used to be a little quirky website that allows travelers to stay in local's houses for a fee. But, soon, it became popular because it provides cheaper and homier accommodations. It also allows travelers to experience cities like a local.

Today, Airbnb established itself as the leader in the short-term rental industry. It has 150 million users as of 2018 and it has more than 600,000 hosts. It also has over four million listing and it's valued at almost $40B. This is the reason why now is the right time to join the short-term rental bandwagon.

Being an Airbnb host comes with a lot of benefits. You get to meet people from all walks of life, so you'll learn more about different cultures. You also get to see your town in the eyes of tourists, so you get to appreciate all the amazing sights in your area. It improves your people skills, too. Plus, it's a great excuse to do overdue home improvements.

But, being an Airbnb host is not as easy as it used to be. Because there are more than half a million other hosts, you must strive to stand out. You must improve your hosting skills and make changes in your home as necessary.

This book is your ultimate guide to becoming an Airbnb superhost. It contains insider tips, strategies, and hacks that you can use to maximize your earnings and achieve success in the short-term rental industry. In this book, you'll learn:

- ✓ What Airbnb is and how it was founded
- ✓ Top things that you need to know before you list your property on Airbnb
- ✓ The characteristics of successful Airbnb hosts
- ✓ How to make your unit "Airbnb ready"
- ✓ Tips that you can use in taking attractive photos of your Airbnb unit
- ✓ How to become a short term rental mogul
- ✓ 22 SEO techniques that you can use to increase your booking
- ✓ How to optimize your listing and increase its visibility
- ✓ How to showcase your USP or unique selling point and increase your bookings
- ✓ How to price your unit competitively
- ✓ 15 photo hacks that you can use to make your property stand out
- ✓ Decorating tips that you can use to improve the aesthetic of your Airbnb unit
- ✓ How to determine your target market
- ✓ The criteria for becoming a superhost
- ✓ 14 superstar host tips that you can use to be one step ahead of your competitors
- ✓ Insider tips that can help you get more bookings and positive reviews
- ✓ What to do when you get a negative review
- ✓ And more!

This book also has various checklists that you can use to improve your home and offer the best amenities. It contains tips and strategies that can help you become a short term rental superstar and increase the earning potential of your home.

So, what are you waiting for? Take a bite from the Airbnb pie and start your journey towards financial freedom and living a balanced life.

Thanks for downloading this book, I hope you enjoy it!

Part I – Airbnb 101

This part of the book talks about everything you need to know about Airbnb – how it was founded, how it can help you earn extra money, things you must know before you become a host, and how to prepare your property.

Chapter 1 – The Perks of Being an Airbnb Host

In 2006, a movie called "The Holiday" was released. It stars Cameron Diaz, Kate Winslet, Jack Black, and Jude Law. The movie is about people swapping houses for the holidays.

The idea seems wild, odd, and somewhat fantasy-like at that time. Why would you allow a stranger to stay in your apartment while you're on vacation? While the movie was amazing, its premise was a bit foolish. It's something that will probably not happen in real life.

But today, The Holiday's premise is no longer outlandish. In fact, more than 600,000 people in the world are renting out their apartments to strangers through a website called Airbnb.

Airbnb and its History

Airbnb is a website which allows property owners to rent out their room, apartment, house, or villa. It allows people to rent out shared spaces, private rooms, or the entire house.

This online marketplace has become more popular in the last years because most of the spaces that you can find in this amazing system are cheaper than hotels. In fact, most travelers can save as much as $35 a day through Airbnb.

Airbnb is also safe and has a wide variety of listings. You can find simple apartment rooms. You could also find luxurious rooms or unique living spaces like castles, art houses, igloos, tree houses, yachts, bungalows, and even penthouses.

Most of all, Airbnb offers you something that a lot of hotels don't – it allows you to live like a local. So, essentially, it gives you a richer and more interesting experience.

Airbnb was founded in 2007 by Brian Chesky, Joe Gabbia, and Nathan Blecharczyk. Brian and Joe are industrial designers who just moved to San Francisco from New York. At that time, both of them were struggling to make ends meet.

That same year, the Industrial Designers Society of America was held in San Francisco. A lot of delegates have a hard time finding a place to stay in, as most hotels were already booked. And so, Brian and Joe bought air mattresses and turned their apartment into a "bed and breakfast".

They soon launched a website called airbnbbreakfast.com, which later became Airbnb. And the rest, as they say, is history.

As of 2018, Airbnb is worth 38 billion dollars. It has more than five million listings and more than 160 million arrivals.

You know what's best about Airbnb? It allows travelers to save a lot of money and it gives an opportunity for locals to make money out of their empty and unused spaces. It's win-win, right? Plus, it boosts the tourism industry, too.

Why You Should Become an Airbnb Host?

Being an Airbnb host comes with a lot of perks, including:

1. *You'll earn extra money.*

Maya used to be a director of a huge IT company in Texas. And so, she earned enough to buy a three-bedroom house in downtown Dallas, but she only uses one room.

After working in the IT industry for 16 years, she decided to quit her job and pursue a childhood passion – writing. It was hard because she was not earning as much as when she was still in the corporate world. So, she decided to list her two empty rooms on Airbnb.

Her listing was in demand because of its amazing location. So, Maya is now earning at least $2900 a month.

Airbnb can be a great source of extra income. It can help you pay off your bills and debts. It also helps you achieve financial freedom and do what you want. You earn more money charging the guests per night that just letting out your property for a monthly fee.

2. *You'll be in control of your time.*

Airbnb is a good source of passive income. This means that you earn money even when you're doing nothing. It essentially helps to retain control over your most valuable asset - your time.

Having an Airbnb business allows you to travel anytime. You are your own boss, so you can choose how to spend your time on things that you are truly passionate about. You don't have to worry about client demands or deadlines. You're free as a bird.

3. *It's a great excuse to renovate and upgrade your home.*

We all want to upgrade our personal space every now and then. But, sometimes, it's just not practical. Being an Airbnb host is a great excuse to give your home a little makeover.

4. You'll meet new people.

Natalie has been searching for love for a long time. After a while, she became at peace with the fact that finding romance may not be in her destiny.

Then, she started renting out her other room. She met new people, explored different places, and became more confident. One day, an Australian surfer named Chris booked her other room. Natalie offered to show him around the city and they eventually fell in love.

One of the best things about being an Airbnb host is that it gives you an opportunity to make new friends and learn about other people's culture. Who knows, you may find love, too.

5. It's a great tool for personal development.

Being an Airbnb host paves way for personal growth, it helps you become more sociable. It also improves your hosting (and even your interior design skills).

You'll also meet demanding and unhappy guests every now and then, so being an Airbnb host also strengthens your patience and customer service skills.

The Major Benefits of Airbnb

Airbnb is probably one of the most marvelous technological creations of the 21st century. It is user friendly. You don't have to be a tech genius to use it. Here's a list of all the other benefits of using Airbnb to rent out your property:

1. It's flexible.

You can choose as to what days the property is available for rental. For example, if you have relatives coming over to stay for a few weeks, you can block off those days on the calendar so you can save the unit for them.

2. You get to know your guests.

When you're running your hotel, you won't get the chance to mingle with your guests and get to know them.

With Airbnb, you can find out a little bit about your guests before they stay at your place. You can also read their reviews and if you get good ones, you'll eventually have regular guests.

3. *The Airbnb market just keeps on growing.*

More people are traveling because airfare has become cheaper over the past few years. So, short-term rental industry keeps on growing.

4. *Airbnb has primary liability coverage of up to $1 million.*

Sometimes the unexpected happens – your cleaner steals your guest's wallet or your guest steals your TV. Don't worry. Airbnb will cover your loss. The company's Host Protection Program covers certain types of property damage.

Airbnb also has your back in case you get sued because your guest got injured while in the bath tub.

Things That You Should Know and Do Before You Become an Airbnb Host

Being an Airbnb host is awesome. It allows you to earn more money and meet new people. It's also a good way to get into the fascinating hospitality and tourism industry.

But, being an Airbnb host is not all butterflies and unicorns. It comes with responsibilities and risks as well. Here's a list of the things that you should remember and consider before you start your Airbnb business:

1. *Check your local laws.*

Airbnb is great, but unfortunately some cities have strict rules regarding Airbnb rentals. For example, if you live in Paris, you can only rent out your flat or apartment for one hundred twenty days a year.

San Francisco allows its residents to rent out their apartments via Airbnb for only up to ninety days a year. Los Angeles also heavily tax hosts.

To avoid fines, imprisonment, or huge fees, you must check your local Airbnb laws before listing your property.

Here's a list of cities with stringent regulations:

- ✓ New York

- ✓ San Francisco
- ✓ Santa Barbara
- ✓ Denver
- ✓ Atlanta
- ✓ Paris
- ✓ Berlin
- ✓ Mallorca
- ✓ Las Vegas
- ✓ Reykjavik
- ✓ Charleston, South Carolina
- ✓ Barcelona
- ✓ Santa Monica
- ✓ New Orleans
- ✓ Tokyo and other cities in Japan

If you live in these cities, it may be risky to put up an Airbnb business.

2. *You should know that there are things that are not covered by Airbnb insurance.*

Airbnb can pay up to $1,000,000 for major property damage. But, you should know that this guarantee doesn't cover certain types of properties, such as artwork, collectibles, and jewelry. You must lock your valuables.

3. *Review your mortgage contract.*

Some mortgage contract prevents you from renting out your home until it's fully paid. So, review your housing or mortgage contract before you list your property on Airbnb. You don't want to have problems with the bank later on.

4. *You have to be clear about what your goals are.*

A lot of people earn huge amounts of money each month on Airbnb. But, it's not the same for everyone. If you just want an extra $200 or $300 a month, you can just invest in clean sheets and towels.

But, if you want to earn more than $1000 a month, your space must be cozy, beautiful, and "Instagrammable". You must also be willing to spend a lot in preparing your unit. You must also be willing to spend a lot of time managing your Airbnb page and entertaining guests.

From the start, you have to be clear about a lot of things. Is Airbnb hosting a side hustle or do you want to make it a full on business? How much do you want to earn from it? How much time can you spare for your hosting? Are you going to rent out your house or are you going to buy new properties for your Airbnb business?

Having clear goals gives you a strong sense of direction. It also helps you to make wiser decisions.

5. *You must be built for hosting.*

Airbnb hosting is not for everyone. To achieve great success on Airbnb, you must be organized. You must be entrepreneurial and you must also have great customer service skills.

You must also be a little sociable and willing to get to know your guests more. You must also be passionate about property maintenance and management.

6. *Find out what kind of host you want to become.*

There are three main types of Airbnb host, so first you have to figure out which one you want to be:

✓ The Opportunist

The opportunist is a host who is only willing to rent out his place only when they are not using it. This type of host is only looking to earn a few hundred bucks from Airbnb. This type of Airbnb is not aiming for continuous success in Airbnb hosting.

✓ Stable Income Host

The stable income host aims to generate a consistent, steady monthly extra income from Airbnb.

This type of host usually has a day job, but wants to consistently generate extra income from his unused spaces and properties.

✓ The Thriving Rentrepreneur

Rentrepreneurs take hosting seriously. They purchase properties for the sole purpose of renting them out on Airbnb and other short-term rental platforms. They also invest a lot of time in designing, decorating, and marketing their units.

Having a clear vision of what you want to achieve as an Airbnb host gives you a strong sense of direction. It helps you make important decisions like how many properties to rent out and how much time you're willing to spend on Airbnb.

7. Understand that Airbnb can be disruptive.

You would have to respond to messages and check on your clients. Plus, there may be a few surprises and emergencies every now and then. Airbnb can disrupt your life in one day or another, so you must be ready for that.

8. Your electricity bills can shoot up.

When you're staying in a hotel, you won't think a lot about conserving energy, right? Well, Airbnb guests don't really care their host would end up with $1000 electricity bill. So, make sure to put signs like "Turn off the lights when you're not using it" or "Turn off the AC/Heater when you're leaving the house".

Don't be impulsive. When you check Airbnb for the first time, you'll instantly find it so enticing that you'll end up listing your property right away. Don't fall into this trap. You have to figure out if short-term real estate property rental is legal in your area. Failure to comply with your local laws can result in huge fines.

Also, you must understand that there will be limitations if you live in a subsidized or rent control building. It's important to check with your property manager, landlord, home owners' association, and the coop board to see what you're allowed and what you're not allowed to do.

Also, you must take note that the income you earn from Airbnb is subject to tax. You also need to consider other costs, such as pool service, landscaping, repairs, utility bills, and cleaning services. So, don't assume that you get to take home everything you earn from this website.

How Much Can You Earn Through Airbnb?

Airbnb is a great way to earn more money. But, how much exactly can you earn through this online marketplace? Well, the answer depends on various factors, such as:

✓ *Location* – The cost of living in a rural area is inexpensive. If your unit is in a rural area, you won't be able to charge much for it. But, if your rental unit is in Philadelphia, Atlanta, Jersey, Santa Barbara, Miami, or Beverly Hills, you can earn thousands of dollars each month.

✓ *The size of your property* – Are you renting out just one room? Are you listing your entire house or are you renting out an entire villa? Your monthly Airbnb income heavily depends on the size of your property.

✓ *The nature of your property* – Do you have a simple English cottage, a studio-type flat, or are you renting a house or a penthouse apartment? Obviously, the rent of a penthouse apartment is way higher than a simple flat that's 30 minutes away from the center of the city.

✓ *The amenities of your unit* – If your unit has great amenities, you'll most likely have great reviews and more people would want to stay in your place.

✓ *Your hosting skills* – Are you reachable and personable? Are you helpful? Do you go an extra mile to provide a great experience for your guests?

✓ *Competition* – If you're living in a place with a lot of hostels and inexpensive hotels, you'll have a hard time maximizing your Airbnb earnings.

To maximize your Airbnb earnings, it's a good idea to rent out an entire house or condo. You should also provide top notch amenities that can give hotels a run for their money. You must also go an extra mile to give your guests an unforgettable experience.

Chapter Recap And Your Action Plan

Airbnb is a great online short term rental platform that you can use to earn money out of your property. Being an Airbnb host comes with a lot of benefits.

But, there are a few things that you must do before you list your property on Airbnb. You must go to your local housing and rental authority and check your city's laws on short-term rental. This will help you avoid huge fines. You must also review your mortgage contract and check with your landlord to avoid problems.

You must also write down your goals. What kind of Airbnb host do you want to become? Do you just want to earn a few hundred bucks or do you want to eventually build a short term rental empire?

Once you're done, place your goal in a visible area. You can place it on your work desk and read it daily. This way, you'll have a clear sense of what you want to achieve as an Airbnb host.

Chapter 2 – How to Get Your Property Airbnb Ready

Preparation is the key to success. You can't just list your property on Airbnb the moment you decide to become a host. You must first think about a lot of things. Who's your target market? What kind of vibe do you want your unit to exude? Are you renting out a room or an entire house? How much are you willing to spend in transforming your unit into a hotel-like paradise? What do you want to offer to your guests?

In this chapter, we will discuss what it takes to be a successful Airbnb host. We'll also discuss a step by step process that you can use to prepare your Airbnb unit.

Do What Works: What Does It Take To Be A Successful Airbnb Host?

Airbnb is a great short-term rental platform. It can help you earn thousands (if not millions) of dollars per year. But, you should know that there's a stiff competition in the hospitality industry. You'll have to compete with B&Bs (Bread and Breakfast), motels, local hotels, and resorts. You also have to compete with a number of other Airbnb hosts in your area. This is the reason why your unit should stand out.

Stay in the local Airbnb units in your area to observe other hosts. You can also stay in Airbnb properties when you're traveling to another city or country. Take note of the things that you like and you don't like in each unit you stay in. This will help you embrace the best practices and avoid the bad ones.

But, you should note that most successful Airbnb hosts offer the following amenities:

1. *Home WiFi* – We all don't want to miss anything while we're traveling, so home Wifi is a must. Also, most people who use Airbnb are digital nomads, so this is a non-negotiable item.

2. *Fireplace* – If you're operating in a cold place like Vancouver, Aarhus, Harbin, or Winnipeg, a fireplace is a plus. This will also significantly reduce your electric bill. A fireplace can also add a lot of aesthetic value to your Airbnb unit. It's also romantic.

3. *Workout equipment* – We live in an Instagram-obsessed world so we all want to look our best. We all want to be fit. This is the reason why it's good to invest in exercise aides and machines.

4. *Coffee-maker* – Who doesn't love coffee? It keeps us awake and it increases our productivity. It also lowers the risk of diabetes. A coffee maker will save your guests a couple of bucks and they'll love you for it.

5. *Desk or working area* – A lot of digital nomads use Airbnb service. So, it's wise to invest in a desk where your guest can have a quiet time with his laptop. Also, make sure to leave a few pens and a pad of paper.

6. *Iron and ironing board* – No one wants to go out wearing wrinkled clothes, right? So, leave an iron and ironing board for your guests. Also leave a note as to where it is and how to use it.

7. *Nightstand and reading lamp* – A lot of people read when they can't sleep so it's great to place a nightstand and a reading lamp next to the bed. Your guests can place their phone or laptop on the bedside table before they go to sleep.

8. *Swimming pool* – Having a swimming pool is definitely a plus. But, if you don't have one, no worries. You can just invest in a bathtub and a backyard sauna.

9. *Heater and air conditioning* – To get those five stars, you must have a "state of the art" HAVC system that can keep your guests warm during winter days and cold during summer days. An efficient HAVC system can save you a lot of money. It improves the airflow in your house and it also increases the resale value of your property.

10. *Television with cable* – There are days when guests just want to stay in their room and watch TV. So, make sure that your unit has a TV and a cable.

11. *Travel-size toiletries* – Travelers have limited luggage space. So, it's a good idea to provide travel-size toiletries that they can use while staying at your place. You can just purchase a few bottles for your guests' shampoo, liquid bath soap, and lotion.

12. *Blankets* – Successful Airbnb hosts usually invest in great blankets. Buy high quality cotton and wall blankets. And, always keep an extra clean blanket, in case your guests will need one.

Successful Airbnb entrepreneurs also have the following common qualities:

1. *They invest in more than one property.*

You can't make a lot of money through Airbnb if you're only renting out one bedroom. Property quantity plays a huge role in your success in the short term rental industry.

Go big or go home. Instead of renting out only one room, you can purchase a few condominium units or holiday houses and rent them out.

2. *They have properties in a great location.*

You can't make a lot of money on Airbnb if your property is not in a tourist destination. So, if you want to be a big and successful short term rental entrepreneur, you should invest in properties in big cities. According to AIRDA, it's best to invest in properties in Chicago, Union City, Miami, Seattle, Astoria, Brooklyn, Honolulu, San Francisco, Cambridge, San Diego, and Washington DC. We will discuss this later on.

3. They have great-looking properties.

Successful Airbnb entrepreneurs understand that having great amenities is simply not enough. Their units usually have high ceiling, patio, amazing view, sauna, marble kitchen counter, and great lighting. Your place must have unique architecture, too.

4. They offer individualized experience.

Successful Airbnb hosts go above and beyond to provide their guests an individualized experience. This means that they do more than list their property details.

They study their guests well and then, they suggest types of local experiences that the guest would like.

Let's take Denise as an example. She lives in a tropical city and rents out two condo units. Before the arrival of her guests, she checks their profile and studies their interests. Then, she prepares a list of places, activities, and restaurants that would suit the preferences of her guests. Because of this, Denise got raving reviews and eventually achieved the superhost status, which we will discuss later on.

Before you even start your journey as an Airbnb host, it is important to observe successful hosts carefully. You have to study them or stay in their unit. This way, you get to adopt their best practices and achieve great success.

How to Prepare Your Airbnb Unit

Once you're already familiar about how Airbnb works and how to be a successful host, it's time to prepare your unit. Below is a step by step guide that you can use to get your place ready for your guests.

Step 1: Determine Your Target Market

It's impossible to please everyone. So, to get good reviews and be a successful Airbnb entrepreneur, you must determine what your target market is. Do you want to attract digital nomads or traveling students? Do you want to cater to families, couples, or solo travelers? Do you want to attract budget travelers or big spenders?

Here's a list of different Airbnb markets that you can focus on:

1. *Couples*

Yep, couple travels are a thing now. So, if you want to target this market, you must have a high quality king bed. Your place must be cozy and also romantic. It can be by the beach or on top of the mountain.

When you're targeting couples, you must expect that a lot of action will happen in your Airbnb unit. So, you have to invest in a cushy bed and high quality comforters.

You can also build a place with terraces and small pool so the guests would feel like they're in their own little private villa.

2. *Solo Women Travelers*

More women are traveling the world alone. Solo travelers usually prefer to stay in an Airbnb unit than in a hotel because it's cheaper. So, this is a good market to target.

A lot of solo women travelers are into Instagram. So, your place must be "Instagrammable". This means that it should look good in photos. You should have nice floral comforters.

You can decorate your house with plastic flowers or indoor plants. It's also a good idea to invest in luxury curtains (women love fabulous curtains).

Leave lavender or ylang-ylang scented toiletries. Women usually like these scents. Also, your place should be clean and safe. Install a door lock that locks from the inside, so your guest will feel safe.

3. Solo Male Travelers

A lot of hosts think that solo male travelers are low maintenance. That's not entirely true. Some solo male travelers can be more demanding and have high accommodation standards.

You could also leave a basketball or better yet, a PS4. Your guest will surely give you a five star review.

4. Digital nomads

Gone are the days when people work solely in the office. Today, a number of writers, IT professionals, bloggers, internet superstars, YouTubers, and marketers have the option to work from home or from anywhere in the world. In fact, a growing number of entrepreneurs also run their business while traveling. These people are called digital nomads.

Digital nomads are always on the go and they are always looking for a cheaper place to stay in. This is the reason why most traveling digital nomads use Airbnb.

To target digital nomads, you must have a strong internet connection with WiFi. It's also important to provide a work desk with a computer, a few pens, and a pad of paper.

Digital nomads don't usually watch TV. As long as there's a computer and an internet, they're good.

Take note that most digital nomads frequently use social media. They usually document their travels. Some of them even post videos of their adventures on YouTube. So, you have to make sure that your place looks good in videos and photos.

5. Group of friends

A lot of people travel in groups. If you want to target travel groups, you must offer an entire condo, house, or villa. You must put a lot of thought into your unit's interior. You must also have multiple beds per room, especially if you're catering to big travel groups.

6. Families

They say that a family that travels together has a tighter bond. Well, that might be true. But, one thing's for sure. More families are exploring the world together.

If you want to target this market, you have to rent out an entire house, villa, or apartment. Your unit must have a spacious living room. You must have a family-sized TV and multiple bathrooms. You must also have a working kitchen and an eight seater dining table.

Your space must be great for kids, too. So, maybe you can include a small indoor tent where the kids can play and sleep. You can also leave a few stuffed toys that the kids can play with.

7. Business travelers

Most business travelers usually book a hotel as they could charge it to the corporate account. But, a lot of them are also starting to use Airbnb.

These people are traveling for work, so they just want something comfy and nice to go home to after a long day of seminars, conferences, trade fairs, or business meetings.

If you're targeting business travelers, keep your unit simple. Use a lot of earth colors. Invest in a few classic furniture pieces and make your unit look like a hotel. It's also important to provide a desk in case your guest needs to work on reports and business presentations.

Create A Prospect Avatar

A prospect avatar is a marketing tool that a lot of successful companies use. It is basically an imaginary person that represents your ideal prospective guest or customer.

Creating a prospect avatar helps you determine your target market. It also allows you to create a marketing campaign that's focused on your prospects.

To create a prospect avatar, you need to think about the characteristics of your prospective guests, including:

- ✓ Age – Do you want to target young students or middle-aged travelers?

- ✓ Education – Do you think your place would attract high school graduates or those with a Master's Degree?

✓ Income level – Do you want to attract ordinary employees or high income entrepreneurs?

✓ Marital status – Is your ideal prospect single or married?

✓ Goals – What's your prospect's goal? Does he wants to save money or does he prioritize quality and superb experience?

✓ Hobbies – Do you want to attract people who like to surf or those who are passionate about crafts or arts? Do you prefer sporty people or beach bums?

✓ Personality – Do you want to attract free-spirited people or the serious, driven ones? What are the hopes and fears of your prospect guests?

Now, after you've identified who your prospective client is, find a photo of a person who matches your ideal prospect on Google. Print the photo and give your avatar a first and last name. Then, write a description of your avatar next to the photo. For example:

"Karla is a 35 year old communication trainer from New York. She's single. She loves to travel. She has a laid back style. She's a hard worker and she likes to just sit by the beach during her free time."

Place the photo and the description on your work desk and look at them each time you're writing a marketing copy for your Airbnb unit.

Step 2: Make Sure That You Have the Best Amenities

You can't get outstanding Airbnb reviews if you're only offering the basic amenities. Before you even list your property on Airbnb, you should make sure that you have the basic amenities that are found in a hotel like clean linens, toilet paper, towels, iron (and full-sized ironing board), and extra keys.

It's also a good idea to leave extra toothbrushes and a hair dryer in the bathroom. This can earn you an extra $10 a night. Also, stock up on high quality shampoos and soaps.

Here's a list of amenities checklist that you can use to provide your guests the best amenities:

1. A high quality bed – This is the most important one. Guests just want to lie down and have a good night's sleep. You must look for a comfortable bed. Invest in a

soft mattress that also provides good support. You must also purchase high quality pillows.

2. Bath towels – You have to provide 2 bath towels per guest. You should also provide beach towels if you own a beachfront unit.

3. Toilet paper – The price of a high quality toilet paper is usually just a few cents higher than the price of the regular one. So, don't skimp on this one.

4. Hair dryer

5. Makeup mirror or a dresser

6. Hand soap

7. Scented shampoo

8. Disposable toothbrush

9. Toothpaste

10. Lotion

11. Disposable razor

12. Note pad

13. Pen

14. Extra linen and pillow cases

15. Tissues

16. Garbage bags and bins

17. Refrigerator

18. Bathroom rug

19. Alarm clock

20. Dishwashing liquid

21. Dust pan, broom, or vacuum cleaner

22. Window and furniture wipes

23. Air spray

24. Pans, pots, plates, forks, spoons, and glasses

25. Magazines and books

26. Cards and board games

27. Cable

28. WiFi

29. Television

30. Adaptors

31. Washing machine

32. Iron and ironing board

33. Fire extinguisher

34. Smoke detector

35. Emergency numbers

36. Maps and guidebooks

37. A first aid kit that includes aspirin, band aids, adhesive tapes, antiseptic wipes, calamine lotion, disposable cold packs, antibiotic ointment, thermometer, and tweezers.

Having great amenities would make you stand out. It will make you a better host and will make you one step ahead of your competitors.

Step 3: Decorate Your Place

You may have to redecorate your place to achieve great success in Airbnb. Here's a list of decorating tips that you can use to transform your place into a homey hotel-like paradise:

1. Choose a theme.

Before you start decorating your place, you need to think of a theme. Do you want your place to look like a hotel or do you want it to feel like a "home away from home"? Do you want your guests to feel like they're in another country?

Below are a few themes that you can use in redecorating and improving your space:

- ✓ Minimalist – The minimalist interior design is getting popular because it's clean and can save you a lot of money, too. If you want a minimalist Airbnb unit, just keep everything simple. Don't use a lot of home décor. Paint your walls white and keep your furniture colors neutral.

✓ Formal Style – This theme exudes elegance. You must adorn your unit with interesting lighting and classic furniture. It also doesn't hurt to use luxury pleated curtains.

✓ Royalty – This is a bit similar to the formal style, but this one is more lavish. So, you must incorporate tasselled curtains, grand chandeliers, and chester sofas.

✓ Boho Chic – This interior design is usually attractive to female travelers. It's fun, colourful, and homey. To achieve this look, you have to invest in items with geometric patterns and tribal prints. You can also incorporate rattan furniture and vintage pieces into your design.

✓ Casual Style – This theme looks cool, casual, and hip. It makes your guests feel at home.

Keep your target market in mind in choosing a theme. If you're trying to attract families or business travelers, having a boho chic theme is not a good idea.

Also, make sure that your unit is unique. The most booked properties are usually those that offer something different to the guests like an unusual architecture, a huge video gaming room, or a rooftop pool.

2. The general rule is to paint your room with neutral colors.

You may have a vibrant and outgoing personality and you want your place to reflect that. Well, that's good. But, remember that you're not the only one staying in your place now.

The general rule is to paint your rooms with neutral colors such as light gray, white, light brown, and beige. This will make it easier for you to attract guests with varying tastes and preference.

If you want to show your personality a little bit to your guests, you can just add bright colored accents such as colourful throw pillows.

3. Mix and match different genres and interior design techniques.

Themed homes are beautiful and captivating. But, they can also get boring. To keep your place interesting, you must mix and match different styles. For example, you can buy a modern sofa set and then use a vintage clock or an electric fan.

You can also have a rustic living room and a modern kitchen. Don't be afraid to mix things up a little bit. Just have fun and let your personality shine through your unit's interior.

4. Invest in good lighting.

Lighting improves the mood of your place. So, put lights in all the right places to enhance the beauty and ambience of your Airbnb unit.

Chandeliers are great because they add aesthetic value to your home. Your kitchen should have enough lighting. You could place a few floor lights to make your home more classy and interesting. Also, consider installing a dimmer in case your guests do not like too much light.

But, remember that there's nothing like natural light. So, make sure that your unit has enough windows. Also use a few mirrors to reflect and maximize natural light.

5. *Use your location as a design inspiration.*

When you're traveling, you usually want to stay in a place that's reminiscent of their destination. For example, if you're traveling to the Maldives, you don't want to stay in a place that looks like a New York Apartment. You'd probably want to stay in a house that reflects the beachy and laid-back lifestyle of Maldives.

If your unit is in a tropical city, try to incorporate some tropic elements into your unit's interior. You can place indoor plants or use tropical-inspired bed sheets. You can also use rattan furniture. You can even install indoor hammocks.

But, if you're living in a big metropolitan city like Brooklyn, you may want to accent your walls with orange bricks and use industrial-style furniture. You can also place a small sculpture of the Statue of Liberty on your coffee table.

Use your location as an inspiration, but don't go overboard. For example, if you live in a jungle, you don't have to use animal print fabrics everywhere.

6. *Consider placing quotes on your walls.*

Wall quotes stickers are fun, inspirational, and they're picture perfect. Also, it's gives your guests a little motivation.

If you want to inspire your guests, place an inspiring quote on one of your walls. Here's a list of motivational quotes you can use:

- ✓ Be the best version of yourself.
- ✓ You can do it.
- ✓ Think happy thoughts.
- ✓ Dream big.
- ✓ Dance like no one is watching.
- ✓ Be grateful.
- ✓ You only fail if you stop trying.

Step 4: Check Your Place to Make Sure That Everything Is Working Well

Before you list your place on Airbnb, you have to go around your property and make sure that everything is working well. You have to check everything from the locks, the faucets, the bulbs, the walls, and the electric outlets.

Conduct a thorough inventory of everything in the house, so you'd know what to charge to your insurance or to the Airbnb Host Guarantee program.

Step 5: Repair What's Broken

You may get a bad review just because your faucet is not working, so repair whatever is broken.

Step 6: Prioritize Your Guests' Safety

The Airbnb insurance is awesome and it's pretty tight. But, to avoid getting into a lot of trouble, you have to make sure that your unit is clean and safe.

Here's a list of safety tips that you can use to improve your guests' overall experience:

- ✓ If you allow guests to bring young kids, make sure to "baby-proof" your house. Make sure that the babies can't reach the TV and other appliances. Also, fasten the electric cords to the wall.

- ✓ Test your appliances and make sure that they are working and functioning properly.

- ✓ Check all the electrical wiring and make sure that they are working and safe. Avoid having loose wires around the house.

- ✓ Make sure that your flat screen TV and book cases are securely bolted to the wall.

- ✓ Use non-slip mats in the bathroom and shower.

- ✓ Place lights outside your home, so you could easily see if there's someone lurking near your house.

- ✓ Always keep an extra light bulb.

- ✓ Remove or repair everything that may pose as a hazard to your guests.

- ✓ Install a separate lock (which locks from the inside) on each room, so your guests will feel safe.

If you have the time, conduct a safety check each time a guest books your place. This is to ensure that your unit is in top notch condition all the time.

Step 7: Conduct an Inventory

Before you list your property on Airbnb, it is important to list everything that's in your unit. This way, you'll also know if something goes missing. Below are the example of the items you need for Airbnb

- Towels (bath and hand)
- Sofa bed
- Mattress and Frame
- Tables (Work/Coffee Tables)
- Soap (Shower and hand)
- Tissue/Toilet/Paper
- Fork/Spoons/Knives/Plates/Cups/Bowl
- TV/TV Stand
- Lamp
- Kettle
- Garbage Can
- Hangers
- Internet

Step 8: Do a Dry Run

Before you list your property on Airbnb, you should conduct a dry run to make sure that everything will go smoothly when you finally welcome guests. Ask a friend to stay in your place and pretend to be a paying customer. Get your friend's honest feedback and then make the necessary adjustments.

Remember that preparation is the most important key to success. You must prepare your Airbnb unit before you open it up to your guests so you'll have great reviews and more bookings in the future.

Chapter Recap and Your Action Plan

To be a successful Airbnb host, you must have superior hosting skills. You must also offer top notch amenities.

Here's an action plan that you can use to prepare your unit and be a superstar host:

1. Check out your competition. Stay in an Airbnb unit in your area or while you are traveling. Take note of your hosts' best practices and copy them.

2. Determine your target market. To do this, you have to create a prospect avatar. Print a photo of your ideal guest and write a short description. Look at this photo each time you're doing marketing for your Airbnb unit.

3. Make sure that your unit has the basic Airbnb amenities, such as shampoo, soap, toilet paper, clean linens, and bath towels. But, if you want to be one step ahead of your competitors, you should also provide a hairdryer, a first aid kit, a working desk, cable, and WiFi.

4. Redecorate your home if you need to. Use neutral colors, but you can add accents like colorful throw pillows or artwork. Don't be afraid to mix and match different design techniques. Also, use your location as an inspiration. If your unit is in a coastal area, you may want to use shells and other beach items as décor.

5. Check your unit carefully and make sure that everything is working well.

6. Repair everything that's broken to protect your clients.

7. Take note of everything that's in the house.

8. Ask a friend to act as a paying customer and ask for an honest feedback.

Don't leave everything to luck. If you want to be a successful Airbnb host, you must take time to prepare.

Chapter 3 – Photos! Photos! Photos! How to Take Great Photos of Your Airbnb Rental Unit

Let's face it – travelers base their booking decisions on the photos they see on Airbnb. Your potential guests may spend a few minutes reading your profile, but they ultimately make decisions based on your property units. This is why it's important that your photos highlight the best features of your property. Here are a few tips that you can use to take amazing photos for your property:

Photo Hack #1: Review the photos of other Airbnb listings to find inspiration

Look at the most booked properties on Airbnb and see how they showcase their property. Don't be afraid to copy the best practices of other hosts.

Photo Hack #2: Use a high quality camera

To really capture the beauty and magic of your unit, it's best to use a high quality DSLR camera. These cameras usually have better image quality. These cameras also allow you to isolate your subject from the background. They work well in both well-lighted and dim environments.

But, it's okay if you don't have a DSLR camera. A lot of cell phone cameras produce great photos, too.

If you're using a cell phone, use the rear-facing camera. This camera takes higher-resolution photos than that front-facing camera.

Photo Hack #3: Keep your target market in mind

Your photos must appeal to the emotions of your target market. If you're targeting couples, you must showcase your place as a honeymoon paradise. You can incorporate champagne flutes and wine in your photos. It's also a good idea to place flowers on the bedside table. Your photos must exude romance and luxury.

If you're targeting families, it's best to show photos of the neighborhood children playing and having fun in front of your unit. You must also take photos of the gate and door locks. You must showcase the safety and family-friendly features of your property.

You must take exciting photos if you're targeting groups of friends. You can take photos of your football table, swimming pool, or billiard table. If you're targeting businessmen, you must showcase premium amenities like a well-stocked pantry, a 45 inch TV, or a breathtaking view of the city.

Photo Hack #4: Set up your place

Your photos must showcase your property in a positive light so you should clean up before your Airbnb photo session.

You must put away the dirty laundry, the dirty dishes, and all the other eyesores. Also, remove your personal items and photos. Remove all the clutter and make sure that your place is squeaky clean. Make the beds and place a few attractive throw pillows.

Here are a few tips that you can use to set up your place:

- ✓ Clean your sinks well.
- ✓ Remove the mould and other deep seated dirt.
- ✓ Highlight the cleanliness of the bathroom.
- ✓ Fold the towels or place them neatly on the towel rack.
- ✓ Place a bag of coffee next to the coffee maker.
- ✓ Put a few books on the coffee table.
- ✓ Arrange the throw pillows on your sofa and couches.
- ✓ Place a few statement pieces.
- ✓ Make your place look comfortable and hospitable.

Photo Hack #5: Showcase your USP or unique selling point

To get more bookings, you must take photos by showcasing a USP or a unique selling point.

But, what is a USP? A USP is your competitive advantage, the thing that sets you apart from your competitors. Does your place have a swimming pool? Do you have a 60" flat screen TV? Is your place located in a touristy area like Athens' Plaka, Milan's Navigli, or San Diego's Little Italy? Does your neighbourhood have a number of street arts?

Airbnb users are most likely to book unique properties. So, highlight the things that make your unit unique such as a grand fireplace, a striking artwork, and a tree house.

Also, take photos of your best amenities, such as patio, hot top, big flat screen TV, entertainment centers, and kitchen.

Take a lot of photos of the bedroom as potential guests would like to know where they're staying and where they're spending most of your time. Make sure that you also take a photo that covers your bedroom furniture – the bed, closet, dresser, and nightstands.

Photo Hack #6: More is more

Airbnb allows you to post 20 photos per listing, so make sure to maximize this limit. Post as much photos as you can. Take the photos of each part of the house – bedroom, basement, kitchen, living room, dining room, game room, patio, backyard, front yard, gate, and most importantly, the bathroom. Before you take photos, make sure that your bathroom is equipped with basic amenities like toilet paper, towel, soap, and shampoo.

Also, take photos of your unit's interior, exterior, and even your frontyard. Take as much photos as you can and then, post the best ones.

Photo Hack #7: Use natural lighting

Avoid using flash. Use natural lighting as much as possible to showcase the innate beauty of your property. This will make your unit more appealing.

Open the windows and lift the shades. This will make each room look lively and warm. Turn on your lamps and lights. Also, take photos during the warmest part of the day, usually around 10 am to 2 pm.

Photo Hack #8: Find the best angle

Look at each room from different angles and take a photo from the best angles. This allows you to showcase the beauty of your property.

Take a wide variety of shots from different angles. For example, you can take a photo of the entire bathroom and then, take another photo of the shell soap holder. Try to focus on different subjects.

Photo Hack #9: Take high resolution photos

The photos must have the resolution of (at least) 1024 x 683px - the bigger the photo, the better.

Photo Hack #10: Take photos in landscape format

Photos are displayed in landscape in search results. This is the reason why you should take your photos in landscape format. This also maximizes your photo space.

Photo Hack #11: Take a lot of photos of the bedroom

Guests want to see the sleeping area, so make sure to take a lot of photos of the bedroom. You can take a photo that captures the entire bedroom and then, you can take other photos that focus on the details and amenities.

Photo Hack #12: Hire a professional photographer if you have to

To showcase your place in the best possible way, it's a good idea to hire a professional photographer. You can hire your favorite local photographer or you can hire one through Airbnb.

All you need to do is log in to your Airbnb account. Go to www.airbnb.com/info/photography and request a photo shoot. Airbnb will then match you up with a professional photographer and schedule the shoot. Make sure that the photographer takes at least three photos of each room so you'll have more options.

Photo Hack #13: Showcase different seasons

If you live in a city that has four seasons, it's wise to take photos that showcase how your property looks like in summer, winter, fall, and spring. Update your photos regularly to showcase the present season. For example, use sunny photos during the summer and then, highlight the snowy backyard or the fireplace during the winter season.

Photo Hack #14: Edit your photos

Edit your photo to make sure that it looks its best. You can use Photoshop or other online photo editing websites, such as:

- ✓ GIMP
- ✓ Photoscape X
- ✓ PIXLR
- ✓ Fotor
- ✓ BeFunky
- ✓ Picmonkey
- ✓ iPiccy

If you use your phone to take photos, you can use picture editing apps, such as Snapseed, VCSO, Afterlight, Enlight, TouchRetouch, and Adobe Lightroom CC.

It's tempting to use filters to make your place look vibrant and more beautiful. But, if you want your place to look attractive, avoid using filters. You want your photos to reflect the true beauty of your property. If you put too many filters on your photos, your guests will be disappointed when they see the real thing. This could lead to bad reviews.

Photo Hack #15: Take Photos of Your Neighborhood

Take photos of your neighborhood, especially if it's one of your unique selling points. Make sure to snap a photo of your village, the stores in the area, or the nearest train station.

They say a photo paints a thousand words, so make sure that your photos tell wonderful stories about your property.

Chapter Recap and Your Action Plan

Photos play an important role in the decision-making process of most Airbnb travelers. This is the reason why you should take attractive photos.

Here are the things that you should do to take great photos:

1. Keep your target market in mind before taking photos. What do they want to see? What do they want to experience? What amenities do they want? For example, if you're targeting digital nomads, you should take photos of the working area. You should also take photos that highlight how quiet the place is.

2. Take as many photos as you can and then choose the best ones.

3. Upload 20 photos that showcase every part in your house – library, living room, dining room, patio, kitchen, basement, attic, front yard, and backyard. Also, include photos of your best amenities and unique selling point like your swimming pool or tree house.

4. Use a high quality camera.

5. Use high resolution photos. The size of the photo should be at least 1024 x 683xp.

6. Don't use your camera flash. Use natural light as much as possible. You must also take photos during day time to maximize light.

7. Clean up your place before you take photos. Remove the clutter and make sure that your unit is in top notch shape.

8. What makes your unit stand out? What are the special amenities that you offer to your guests? Airbnb travelers like to book unique properties. This is why you should highlight your unique selling point or USP.

9. Hire a professional photographer if you have to.

10. Showcase different seasons so the guests would see what your property looks like during fall, winter, spring, and summer.

Having great photos is essential in increasing your bookings and Airbnb earnings.

Chapter 4 – Creating Your Listing

After taking photos of your property, it's time to create your listing. Airbnb is an online community of short term rental entrepreneurs and travelers. This is the reason why both guests and hosts are asked to create a personal profile. This way, guests can make an informed decision about which property to book. This also gives the hosts the opportunity to review the guest's profile before accepting the requested reservation.

Your Airbnb account has different components, which includes your personal profile, your property listing, photos of your unit, your profile picture, your personal ratings and reviews, and your property ratings and reviews.

Remember that your profile page includes a summary of the reviews you have received both as a host and a guest. So, if you were a bad and messy guest in your past travels, your potential guests will also see this information. So, you should strive not only to become a good host, but also a reliable and neat guest.

Sign Up for the Airbnb Service

To create your short term rental account, you must go to http://www.airbnb.com/c/rwong102?currencyHKD and then, click on the "sign up button". If you're using a smartphone or a tablet, you have to download the app. You can sign in using your email, Facebook account, or your Google account.

Add Your Profile Information

To create your profile information, you must do the following:

1. Add your profile photo. It's best to choose a photo of you wearing a business outfit, standing in front of your property. This increases your credibility.

2. Add and confirm your phone number.

3. Choose your preferred language. You should also add your preferred currency (US dollars if you're from the United States).

4. Specify your location. You don't have to add your street name at this point. You can just place your city, state, and country.

5. Place your education. This is optional information, but you should fill this out anyway. This helps you to get to know your guests a little bit more.

6. Place your job under "work field". You can be as broad as possible.

7. Add your time zone. Also, you must specify the languages you speak. This allows you to attract international travelers.

8. Add emergency contact details and shipping information.

You must also add photos and symbol. You must also verify your profile. We will discuss this step later on. You should also add character references later on.

Create Your Airbnb Property Listing

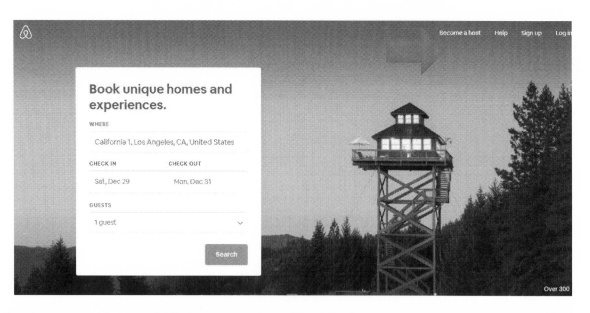

After you created your Airbnb personal profile, it's time to create your property listing. To do this, you must go back to the Airbnb homepage, sign in to your account, and click on "Become a Host" button.

Your property listing should have the basic information about the property, including bathrooms, bedrooms, beds, and other amenities. It should also include the photos of your property and an attention-grabbing and creative title.

Your property listing must also include your nightly price and other booking-related information. You can also add optional items, such as a Host Guidebook. Below is a step by step guide in creating a property listing.

Step 1 – Add Basic Information About Your Listing

After you click the "become a host" button, you'll need to ask a number of questions, including:

- ✓ What type of property you're listing? – Are you listing an entire house, a shared room or a private room?

- ✓ How many guests can you accommodate?

- ✓ How many bathrooms do you have? – You must also indicate if the guest has access to a private bathroom or if he will have to use a shared bathroom.

- ✓ What amenities do you offer? – Check the box of the amenities you offer.

- ✓ What spaces can guests use? – Specify what type of rooms your guests have access to. Do they have access to the gym, hot tub, parking, elevator, or kitchen?

- ✓ Where's your place located? – You have to put your complete address, including the street name, city, state, country, and zip code.

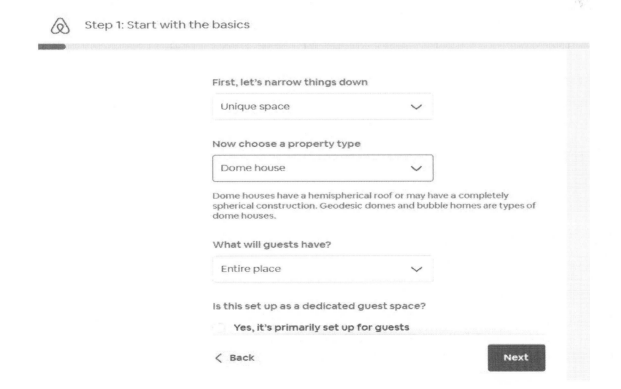

Don't forget to update your profile in case you decide to rent out more rooms or provide more amenities.

Step 2: Take Photos of Your Unit and Add Description

The next step is to take photos using the tips in Chapter 3. Once you're done, you will have to fill out three fields, namely:

1. Point of Interest (My place is close to ...) – Is your property located in an artsy area? Is it near a tourist spot or a popular restaurant? Is it just a few steps away from a popular shopping mall?

2. Your USP or Unique Selling Point (You'll love my place because of ...) – What makes your place special? Is it the ambience, the neighbourhood, the people, or the architecture?

3. Your Target Market (My place is good for ...) – What type of traveler do you cater to? Do you cater to solo adventurers, couples, adventurers, business travelers, big groups, or families? Do you also cater to those traveling with pets?

Airbnb will draft a one paragraph, text-based description based on your USP, target market, and unique selling point. You can edit this and add a personalized and attention-grabbing 500 character description. We will discuss tips that can help you write an awesome property description in the later part of this chapter.

Step 3: Set Your Nightly Rate and Your Available Dates

Remember that the short-term rental industry is quite competitive. This is the reason why you should also set competitive prices.

Before you set your nightly price, you must do an extensive research. Check the prices of the Airbnb listings in your area. You must also check the rates of nearby hotels, bed & breakfast, resorts, and motels. You can charge a higher nightly rate if you're in a high-demand location.

You have two pricing options – fixed pricing and smart pricing. If you decide to choose the Smart Pricing option, Airbnb will determine the price based on your location. The system automatically increases the rate on high demand nights. This maximizes your revenue.

If you choose the fixed rate, you get to choose your nightly rate. The rate will stay the same unless you decide to change it.

On your first few months, it's wise to set your nightly price a little bit lower than most of your competitors to increase your bookings and build your reputation. You can gradually increase your nightly rate once you established yourself as a reliable and trustworthy host.

Setting a low nightly rate is a wise thing to do, especially if you are still a beginner. But, make sure that you are still earning profit. You must consider the following costs in setting the right price:

- ✓ Mortgage payment
- ✓ Insurance
- ✓ Property tax
- ✓ HOA fees
- ✓ Maintenance fee
- ✓ Cleaning service fee
- ✓ Airbnb fee (3%)

You must also go to the calendar to set your property availability. You can block out specific dates. You can also use the "trip length" option to set the maximum and minimum number of consecutive booking days. For example, you can set a two-night minimum stay to maximize your revenue.

As a new host, you should keep your maximum stay period to just one week. You don't want to end up having someone staying in your place for months in case you decide to stop being an Airbnb host.

You should also set the following:

- ✓ Advance notice – This is the number of days your guests have to book and pre-pay before arrival. You should require at least one day advance notice so you have enough time to prepare your unit.

- ✓ Preparation time – How much time do you need in between reservations to prepare and clean your unit?

- ✓ Booking – How far can a guest book a reservation? Is it any time, three months, six months, or one year?

Step 4: Request Extra Guest Information

Your guests should provide basic information such as profile photo, contact number, payment information, and email address.

You can also request additional information from your potential guests such as government-issued IDs and recommendations from other hosts. You can also choose "no additional reviews" as a requirement.

You can also turn off the "instant book" option so you can screen your guests. But, when you do this, be prepared to respond to reservation requests within an hour or two. Otherwise, you'll lose the reservation to someone else.

<u>Step 5: Create Your House Rules</u>

To protect yourself and your property, be clear about what you will and will not accept. This is the reason why you should set house rules.

If your guests break your house rules, you have the option of cancelling their reservation (without penalty). You can also ask your guests to leave.

Below is a list of rules that you can use as a guide in writing your own house rules:

1. No pets allowed – Even if you're a pet lover, it's best to ban pets to protect your property. You don't want your place to smell like dog urine. But, you can charge a premium rate if you decide to allow pets.

2. No parties – Parties are messy and they could result to property damage and complaints.

3. No illegal activities – There are horror stories of guests using Airbnb properties to shoot porn or as a brothel. So, it's necessary to include this item in your house rules.

4. No drugs – This is a must. You don't want your place to be a hub for coke-heads and stoner kids.

5. No visitors – You don't want your property to become a "hookup" hub.

6. No smoking – You can ban smoking and if you allow it, you can just specify the parts of the house where your guests are allowed to smoke like in the patio.

7. No eating in the bedroom – You don't want your bedroom to be filled with ants. So, it's important to add this item in your house rules.

You should also specify quiet hours, cleaning procedures, and off-limit areas. You must also print a copy of your house rules and place it in the fridge or any visible area in your property.

How To Create An Attention-grabbing Listing Title

Your property title looks like a headline and it's the next thing your potential guests will see after your main photo.

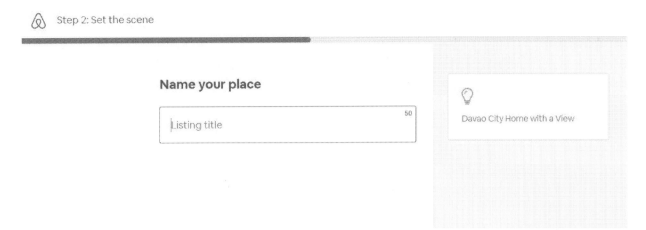

The goal of your title is to get readers to click on your property link and view your listing. This is the reason why it should be catchy and unique.

Here are a few tips that you can use in writing your title:

1. Maximize the entire 50 character space. Use as much space as you can.

2. Create a title that appeals to your target market. Don't use generic words. Try to narrow down your focus. For example, if you're trying to target business travelers, you can add your location. You can also use words like convenient or modern.

3. Do not use generic words, such as "good" or "nice". Use more descriptive words such as "country chic", "rustic", or "minimalist".

4. Mention the best features of your place like a hot tub or a pool.

5. Include your location and your landmark. You could mention that your unit is near a train station, a mall, or a tourist spot. Most travelers opt for convenience so they likely book properties that are near restaurants and high-rise buildings. This will make your title SEO-friendly, too. We will discuss this later on in this book.

6. Use abbreviations. Remember that your title should be at least 50 characters. This is why you should use abbreviations, such as AC (air conditioning), BR (bedroom), or w/ (with).

7. Include your USP or unique selling point in your title. It could be a pool, amazing sunset view, or its unique architecture.

8. Use symbols like ★. This will make your title stand out.

9. Update your title regularly and highlight upcoming events. For example, if your place is just ten minutes away from this year's Coachella, include that in your title.

Below is a list of compelling titles that you can use as a guide:

- ✓ Stunning 4 BR old cottage w/ sunset view + pool
- ✓ Luxury 2 BR condo in shopping area w/city view
- ✓ 5 BR Victorian mansion overlooking Lake Como
- ✓ Newly renovated 2 BR townhouse w/kitchen + pool★
- ✓ Rustic beach house w/pool for honeymooners
- ✓ Charming old cottage 5 mins from Swiss Alps ★
- ✓ Spacious 2 BR condo w/view of the Acropolis
- ✓ Comfy 1 BR flat w/fireplace + wifi + cable
- ✓ 1 BR modern aprtmnt w/wifi, private bathroom ★

Keep your Airbnb title short and interesting and eye-catching. Remember the goal is to encourage your reader to click your link and read your entire listing.

Tips on Creating a Striking and Irresistible Listing Description

One of the best ways to increase your bookings is to write a compelling property description. Airbnb drafts a listing description based on the information you enter into the system. But, you can edit this and make your own 500 character description. This description is called listing summary.

The Listing Summary

This gives your potential guests an overview of what to expect from the property. It has to be 500 characters long (or less). It also has to be well-written and eye catching.

Here are a few tips that you can use to write your listing summary:

1. Answer your potential guests' questions before they even ask.

To write a great copy for your listing, you have to think like a guest. If you were a guest, what do you want to know about the property?

Your description should answer your prospective guests' questions before they ask, like:

- ✓ How far is your place from the train station?

- ✓ Is there a mall or a shopping district in your neighborhood?
- ✓ What type of beds do you offer? Do you offer twin beds or a huge king bed?
- ✓ Can your guests bring their pets?
- ✓ Can your guests hold a birthday party in your country chic chateau?
- ✓ Does your room have a private bathroom?
- ✓ Does your rental unit have a separate entrance?

2. You should write a description that's appealing to your target audience.

Use words that appeal to the emotions of your audiences. For example, if you're attracting business people, use the words "luxury" and "convenience". Use words like "budget-friendly" and "value for your money" for backpackers. Also, use the words "safe", "secure", and "child-friendly" if you are trying to attract families.

You should write a detailed description that's emotionally appealing to your target audience. For example:

- ✓ If want to attract business travelers, you must mention how near your place is to the business center. You should also mention that your place has a reliable WiFi connection and a quiet work area. You can write something like:

  "This one bedroom condominium is located at the heart of the city's business district. It is equipped with strong wifi connection and it has an office area that you can use to work on reports. It also has a pantry equipped with a high quality coffee machine."

- ✓ To target couples, you must mention the romantic vibe of your property. You must also focus on the overall ambience of the bedroom. You can write something like:

  "This beachfront villa is perfect for honeymooners. It's nestled in a beautiful beach town, surrounded with palm trees. The bedroom has a Victorian interior. It has a luxurious queen bed that makes you feel like a royalty. It also has a wooden dresser and an intricately carved nightstand."

- ✓ If you're targeting families, you must highlight your kid-friendly spaces. You can write something like:

  "This two bedroom house has a spacious playroom and an outdoor area, a perfect bonding area for the whole family."

3. Highlight your unique selling point.

As with your listing title, you must also showcase your listing's unique selling point in your description. Be detailed and descriptive as possible. For example:

> *"This five bedroom villa has a spacious rustic veranda that overlooks the breathtaking city skyline."*

> *"The kitchen has a marble counter that you can use in preparing your meals. It's also equipped with top of the line amenities including a four burner stove, an oven, a two door refrigerator, a spacious cupboard with high quality glassware, a coffee machine, and a rice cooker."*

4. Do not use cheap words.

You have to use well-thought words if you want your listing to stand out. Avoid cheap words like good, great, nice, or awesome. Hyperbolic language isn't as convincing as it once was. Why? Because everybody says that their property is the best.

To increase your bookings, you must be specific. Instead of saying "awesome view", say something like "the master bedroom offers a glimpse of the city's sparkling skyline".

Other Listing Description Spaces

Aside from the summary, there are also a number of optional "description sections", including:

About Your Space

This is where you describe your listing. If you're renting out the entire property to your guests, write a description for each room. Why? So, guests can plan sleeping arrangements ahead. This also allows your guests to plan an efficient and budget friendly itinerary.

For example, if you write a detailed description of all the appliances in your kitchen, your guests can opt to cook food instead of eating in expensive restaurants.

Below is an example that you can use as a guide:

"The living room:

The living room has a modern interior with a sofa and two Chesterfield chairs. It exudes comfort and elegance. It has a fireplace that keeps you warm during cold nights and a 45" flat screen TV.

The kitchen:

The kitchen has a spacious dining area where you and your travel buddies can enjoy meals together. It has amenities, such as:

- ✓ *Four burner oven*
- ✓ *6 seater dining table*
- ✓ *Griller*
- ✓ *Knives, plates, saucers, plates, spoons, and forks*
- ✓ *Full-sized dishwasher*
- ✓ *Paper towels*
- ✓ *Coffee machine*
- ✓ *Rice cooker*

This vacation home has three bedrooms, namely:

Room 1: Master bedroom with king-sized bed, dresser, nightstand, TV, bathroom, spacious walk-in closet, and balcony that overlooks the city.

Room 2: Large room with one double deck bed and one queen sized bed. It can accommodate up to four people. It also has a bathroom and a closet.

Room 3: A small bedroom with two twin beds. Guests who stay in this room can use the hallway bathroom. It's great for kids."

<u>Your Interaction with Guests</u>

This space describes your interaction with your guests. This is a great opportunity to let your guests know that you won't be around most of the time and that you respect their privacy. But, you should also let them know that they can contact you in case they need anything.

You could say something like:

"We have a "self check-in" lock box. But, you can contact our host anytime. He has been travelling around Bali and can give you inside information about the best spots in the city including restaurants, exclusive bars, bike rentals, gyms, beaches, and even yoga studios."

<u>What Your Guests Can Access</u>

You don't have to do this if you are renting the whole property. But, if you are only renting out one room, then you should specify what your guests can access.

You can mention share areas such as the living room, the kitchen, backyard, patio, or the pool. You must also mention the areas that are off limits to the guests like your daughter's playroom or the library.

Details about Your Neighborhood

Airbnb users book properties that are in a good neighborhood. This is the reason why you should write about the safety and beauty of your neighborhood. Do you live in a gated community? Is the area well-lighted? Is it accessible? How far is the nearest bus stop or train station? Are there malls and grocery stores in your area?

Also, try to include five interesting places in your neighborhood. Here's an example that you can use:

"Carrie's homestay is located in Seminyak, right at the heart of the beautiful island of Bali. It is just 35 minutes away from the airport.

There are a lot of things that you can do in this place. You can ride horses and go surfing on the Seminyak Beach. A sea temple called Pura Petitenget is just a few minutes away.

You can spend your nights in a beachfront bar called Ku De Ta. You can do yoga at Seminyak Yoga Shala and you can shop at a shopping haven called Jalan Laksmana."

How to Get Around the House

You can skip this one if you're not renting out a villa with ten bedrooms and four floors.

Other Things to Note

This is your opportunity so include a "call to action" to urge your readers to book your property.

Remember that if guests read your description up to the end, it means that they are interested. They just need a little nudge. This is why you should write an interesting closing sentence that would encourage your readers to send you an inquiry or book your unit.

You can write something like:

- *"The calendar has been filling in fast, so send me a message to secure your reservation."*
- *"I am excited to host you and your travel buddies. Send me a message now."*
- *"If you are traveling on a budget, just send me a message and maybe we can come up with a deal."*

You should also include the check in and the check-out time in this section.

Your listing description is a tool that you can use to increase your bookings. So, make sure that it's well-written. Write a draft, read what you've written carefully, and don't forget to edit.

Once you're ready, upload your photos and voila, your career as an Airbnb host has officially begun.

Chapter Recap and Your Action Plan

Before you can start earning money from Airbnb, you need to create an account. Once you're done, you can create your listing.

Here's a list of things that you have to do to create your Airbnb listing:

1. Sign up for the service at www.airbnb.com. You can sign up using your email, Facebook, or Instagram account. Remember that you're going to use this account both as a guest and as a host.

2. You need to add your profile information such as your profile photo, contact number, preferred language, location, education, time zone, line of work, and emergency contact details.

3. To create your property listing, you need to hit the "become a host button". You should also add some basic information about your listing. You need to add your description. Then, determine your nightly rate. You can also request extra guest information if you are keen in screening your guests.

4. Create your house rules to protect yourself and your property. You have to be clear about what you expect from guests.

When you're writing your listing description, try to utilize all the space that Airbnb provides. Describe each room and don't forget to highlight your best amenities.

Part II – Increase Your Bookings and Become a Superhost

The second part of the book talks about what a superhost is and why you should aspire to be one. It also tackles marketing and SEO strategies that you can use to increase bookings. This part also talks about how you can always be one step ahead of all your competitors and become a superstar host.

Chapter 5 – What is A Superhost and Why You Should Aspire to Be One?

A superhost is an experienced Airbnb host who provides extraordinary and top-notch experiences for their guests. These hosts usually get a five-star rating from their guests. It's a designation for hosts that meet certain criteria.

If you're serious about earning a lot of money on Airbnb, you should aspire to become a superhost. Why? Well, it increases your Airbnb earnings faster and it also builds your credibility. It helps you attract more guests, too.

Being a superhost is not that hard to achieve. You just have to be an amazing host and pass certain criteria.

Superhost Criteria

To become a superhost, you must meet the following criteria:

1. You must have completed ten bookings or three long term reservations that total to at least one hundred nights a year. For example, if you have four clients who stayed in your place for at least 30 days each then you're qualified. If you're really good, you'll become a superhost in less than six months.

2. You have at least 50 percent review rate. This means that at least half of your guests must post a review.

3. You must have a ninety percent response rate. This is why you should respond to all inquiries and messages on the Airbnb system.

4. You must have zero cancellations, except in extenuating circumstances such as death in the family, serious illness, jury duty, court appearances, travel restrictions, military deployment, airport closure, road closure, or severe property damage.

5. You must have a rating of at least 4.8.

You don't need to apply to become a superhost. Airbnb usually conduct a quarterly assessment for each host. If you meet the criteria, Airbnb will notify you of your superhost status approximately ten days after the assessment.

Why You Should Aspire To Become a Superhost?

Superhosts are more credible. First time Airbnb users are most likely to book units owned by superhosts.

Plus, having a superhost status allows you to book more frequently and charge a little bit more.

Here are a few benefits of having a superhost status:

1. Superhosts also get priority support. This means that they get fast-tracked through the queue. Their issues are dealt with quicker and faster.

2. A lot of Airbnb guests use the superhost filter. This means that they can only see superhosts. So, having a superhost status can give you access to a picky group of guests. This translates to more bookings and increased revenues.

3. People who can maintain their superhost status for a year get a travel coupon worth one hundred dollars. They can spend this on their own Airbnb vacation.

4. Superhosts usually get invited to exclusive Airbnb events or new feature launches.

Also research shows that superhosts earn more than twenty percent more than regular hosts.

Basic and Insider Tips That Can Help You Become a Superhost

Becoming a superhost is not that hard. Below is a list of both basic and insider tips that you can use to achieve the superhost status.

Schedule Your Airbnb Time

You must have at least 90 percent response rate to become a superhost. This means that you should be able to respond to most of your messages within the 24 hour window. This is a bit challenging, especially if you have a day job.

The best way to achieve a high response rate is to incorporate your Airbnb response time into your schedule. For example, you can respond to Airbnb messages daily from 8:00 am to 9:00 am and from 7:00 pm to 8:00 pm. This will increase your response rate and improve your guests' experience.

Also, if you're traveling and you do not have access to the internet, you can set up an auto response system via <u>Superhost Tools</u>. This system helps you manage and automate your Airbnb listing. This tool has awesome features like:

- ✓ Auto Review – This allows you to automatically review your guests (with a five star rating) after check out. This system also sends a message to your guests to let them know that you left a five star review.

- ✓ Auto Messaging – You can use this feature to send your guests automated (and yet personalized) messages.

- ✓ Multiple Listings – This feature allows you to manage multiple listings.

The point of being an Airbnb entrepreneur is to have full control over your time. So, you have to manage your time well. Schedule your Airbnb time and automate some tasks if necessary.

Fill in Your Host Profile

Filling up your host profile is the first step to becoming a superhost. Having an intensive and detailed profile increases your credibility. It also gives you an opportunity to position yourself as a competent, accommodating, and extraordinary host. Here's how you can do that:

Step 1 – Verify Your Offline ID

This step allows you to establish yourself as a trustworthy, reliable, and credible host. When you do this, Airbnb checks your identity against a government-issued ID to make sure that all your info is correct.

To do this, go to your "profile settings". Then, go to the "Trust and Verification" tab, and then, you'll need to send Airbnb a scanned copy of your government-issued ID.

Step 2 – Post an Interesting Description of Yourself

Having an interesting personal description improves your likeability as a host and increases your bookings. Your personal description is only 73 characters long, so you have to choose your words well.

Use the personal description part to describe your interests and showcase your skills as a host. Here's an example that you can use as a guide:

"I have extensive experience in the hospitality industry. I have been an Airbnb host for five years now. I currently own five Airbnb units – 4 condos and a three-bedroom tropical villa. I have hosted more than a hundred people and still counting. I am passionate about giving my guests an extraordinary experience. I am approachable, organized, and driven. I invest a lot of time and effort in my rental units."

Remember to keep your description professional yet fun and interesting. Also, keep it as short and direct to the point as you can.

Step 3 – Upload an Interesting, but Professional Profile Image

It's a good idea to upload your updated photo on your profile page if you want to increase your bookings and become a superhost.

Remember that Airbnb is not a dating site and definitely not your regular recreational social networking site. So, do not post photos of you skydiving or playing with your dog. It's best to post a photo of you sitting in your unit's living room or standing in front of your house.

You can also post a photo of you wearing a crisp three piece suit. If you're running a short-term rental company, you can post the photo of the team responsible for designing, decorating, and managing your properties.

Step 4- Fill Out the "About Me" Section

The "about me" section gives you an opportunity to describe yourself and give your guests an idea of who you are and what you like. You can place interesting facts about you like your alma mater, hobbies, and the languages you speak.

Below is an example that you can use as a guide:

"I am Emily. I am a mom to two wonderful kids and a wife to an amazing man. I have a degree in Business Management. I have extensive experience in real estate and hospitality industry. I love to travel that's why I'm passionate about providing high quality and comfortable rooms to other travelers. I have been to 23 countries and 56 cities."

Step 5- Provide References

You have the option to add references, people who can speak highly of you and your properties. Your references can be a social proof that you can use to increase your credibility.

You can request two of your trusted friends to put in a good show for you. Ask them to write references that highlights your professionalism, honesty, reliability, and friendliness.

Step 6 – Create A Strategic Wish List

Create a wish list that includes clean and high quality properties. This shows your guests how important cleanliness is to you.

Be Honest

It's great to put your unit in a positive light, but don't exaggerate. Be honest when posting your photos and descriptions. For example, don't say that your place has a pool if it doesn't have one. You have to set proper expectations.

Keep your photo editing at a minimum. It's important to write a great marketing copy, but do not try to oversell your products. And most importantly, don't make promises that you cannot keep.

Debunking the Myths about Airbnb Superhost Status

A lot of people think that becoming a superhost is a difficult feat that requires a lot of time and money. But, that's not entirely true. Here are the most common myths about being a superhost:

1. You can't have a day job because you are on-call "24/7".

You don't have to attend to your Airbnb account 24 hours a day, seven days a week. In fact, a lot of successful superhosts have a day job. Some of them are accountants, lawyers, and even doctors.

There are a number of third party tools that you can use to automate your account. You can also manage your time by incorporating your daily Airbnb tasks into your schedule.

2. You must have a lot of properties to become a superhost.

It's true that having a lot of properties can earn you a lot more money. But, you don't need to have multiple units to be a superhost.

You can become a superhost even if you only have one listing as long as you have at least 10 bookings a year (which should sum up to 100 days).

3. You cannot cancel a listing.

Normally, you should have zero cancellations to achieve the superhost status. However, there are exemptions. Airbnb allows you to cancel a booking in case of certain justifiable circumstances, such as political unrest, natural disaster, death in the family, serious property damage, and serious illness.

Can I Lose My Superhost Status?

Yes. Airbnb hosts are evaluated four times a year and if you don't maintain your rating and your review rate until the next review period, Airbnb can take away your superhost status.

To maintain your superhost status, you must continue to meet the requirements every assessment period.

Chapter Recap and Your Action Plan

A superhost is an elite Airbnb host who's known for delivering exceptional service to his guests. Superhosts usually get priority support. Their listings are also more visible, so they have more bookings and earnings than regular people. Here are a few things that you should do to become a superhost:

✓ You must have at least three bookings per year. These bookings must amount to 100 days. This means that your place should be booked for one hundred days per year.

✓ You must encourage your guests to write a review because you must have at least 50 percent review rate to become a superhost. One of the best ways to do this is to give your guests a good review right after they leave. This will encourage them to return the favor.

✓ You must have a response rate of ninety percent. This means that you must respond to almost all of your messages within 24 hours. The best way to do this is to schedule your Airbnb response time twice daily – in the morning and at night. This technique will help you manage your time as well.

✓ You should also fill in a host profile. Verify your offline ID to increase your credibility. You should also look like a professional in your photo. If you manage multiple listings, you should use the photo of your design and maintenance team as a profile picture.

- ✓ Cast yourself in a positive light, but do not exaggerate. Be honest.

- ✓ Do not cancel a listing except when you're extremely sick, someone died in your family, or there's a natural disaster.

If you want to earn a huge amount of money on Airbnb, you should aspire to be a superhost. Being a superhost increases your credibility and bookings. It also comes with a few cool rewards. Plus, it's a great source of pride.

Chapter 6 – Optimize Your Listing: Use SEO techniques to Increase Your Bookings

To become a superhost and maximize your booking, your place must be booked for at least 100 days a year. To tell you the truth, this is not easy to achieve. This is the reason why you should employ SEO strategies to increase your listing's visibility and increase your bookings.

Airbnb is ultimately a search engine that uses a "search ranking algorithm" to help guests find the best listing for their trip. If you're not on the first few pages of the Airbnb search results, you're less likely to get bookings.

So, to make it easier for guests to find you, you must employ an internet marketing strategy called SEO or search engine optimization. This strategy aims to increase your ranking on Airbnb results, making your listing more visible to potential guests.

Here's a list of SEO tips that you can use to optimize your listing and get more bookings:

SEO Hack #1: Place your location in your Title and Description

Airbnb works like Google. Guests usually type the location in the search bar. So, your listing's ranking will go higher in Airbnb results if your title includes your location.

It's also a great idea to include appealing keywords that are relevant to your location, such as tourist attractions, landmarks, and festivals.

SEO Hack #2: Make your listing stand out

Guests are usually looking for a high quality place to stay in. This is why you have to make your effort stand out. You must use powerful descriptive words. Your main listing photo must also showcase your best amenity like the beautiful beachfront exterior or the romantic bedroom.

SEO Hack #3: Respond to the inquiries as fast as you can

If you're a guest, you'd get seriously pissed if you contact a host and you get a response a month later? This is why Airbnb search algorithm rewards those who respond to the guests quickly.

So, to get to page 1 of the search results, you have to reply to your guest's messages as soon as you can. You don't have to provide a complete reply. You can just say "Thank you for your query, I'll get back to you as soon as I can".

SEO Hack #4: Update your calendar regularly

You're most likely to get ranked in the search results if your listing is accurate. This is why you should update your daily pricing and calendar availability regularly (if possible, daily).

SEO Hack #5: Get five star ratings

Airbnb want to deliver great service to its users, this is why well-rated listings usually rank first.

To increase your bookings you must make sure that you get good ratings and give amazing service to your guests.

Also, don't forget to email your guests right after they leave. You have to actively ask for critical feedback. You have to let them know that you're serious about improving your services. Tell them that their feedback is critical to your success.

Also, don't forget to leave your guest a review. Guests are more likely to write you a review if you review them first.

SEO Hack #6: Create a guidebook

Airbnb allows you to create a basic handbook for your guests. This handbook includes popular tourist destinations, shopping areas, and restaurants.

You see, Airbnb users usually search for landmarks, neighborhoods, and tourist traps, so including popular destinations in your listing will increase your visibility in the search engine results. We will discuss more about this guidebook later on.

SEO Hack #7: Reduce your minimum night requirement and increase your maximum night

If you want your listing to show up in the maximum number of searches, you have to reduce the minimum nights. You should also increase your maximum nights limit.

Why? Because the Airbnb algorithm prioritizes listings with low minimum night and high maximum night limit.

But, if you're a new host and you're not sure if you want to do this in the long run, you may want to keep your maximum night limit to one week. This way, you won't get stuck with guests who want to stay in your place for six months.

SEO Hack #8: Offer a monthly discount

Airbnb also wants to cater those who rent apartments for more than 29 days. So, if you want your listing to appear in a lot of searches, you must offer a monthly discount on top of your base rate.

To do this, you need to go to your listing. Then, click on "manage listing". Click on "pricing". Then, edit the "length of stay prices". Enter the amount of your monthly discount. Providing monthly discounts can help you attract long-term guests.

SEO Hack #9: Enable the "instant booking" feature

Instant booking is a feature that allows guests to book a property immediately. Because most travelers like to book a room quickly, this feature also increases your reservations.

Using this feature keeps you from screening your guests. But, it also increases your listing's visibility. So, you have to make a choice. Do you want to be able to choose your guests or do you want to rank in the Airbnb search engine?

SEO Hack #10: Check out the top Airbnb earners in your area and find out what their keywords are

Go to AirDNA. Type your location in the search bar and go to "top properties" to see the top earners. Then, check out the "keywords" that the top-earning listings use.

You'll see that if you type the location "San Francisco", you'll see that top listings use keywords like "near Hollywood", "villa", "retreat", and "view".

SEO Hack #11: Incorporate nature's gift into your photos

You must present your property in the best possible light. The best way to do this is to incorporate natural views into your photos. For example, if you're living in a mountainous area, take photos during the summer or spring time, so you can capture the beauty of the leafy trees. If you live in an island, it's best to post a photo of your home's sunset view.

SEO Hack #12: Your Cover Photo Must Exude the Overall Vibe of Your Location

Travelers are most likely to book a property that exudes the vibe of the place they're traveling to. This is the reason why your listing cover photo must exude the vibe and the allure of your location.

For example, if you're renting out a Las Vegas condominium, your cover photo must capture the brilliance, brightness, and glitter of the entire city.

If you're renting out a villa in Bali, your photo must capture the beauty and laid-back vibe of the island.

Walk to the
Beach from a
Secluded Oasis

A haven of tranquillity on the Island of the Gods. A seamless blend of concrete floors, vaulted ceilings, and open walls creates a stylish tropical retreat rippling with character. The funky kitchen showcases faded retro tiles.   2 min walk to beach.

"Just can't beat going for a quick swim or surf at the beach in the morning."

SEO Hack #13: Your listing description must be scannable

The "about space" section doesn't have a limit, but you should note that Airbnb users do not have all the time to read a long description. This is why you should make your description scannable.

To do this, follow these tips:

- ✓ Use interesting words.

- ✓ Use bullet points. Don't be afraid to enumerate the benefits. Also, don't be afraid to use hyphens (-), plus signs (+), and an arrow (→). These characters make your description more scannable and easy to read.

- ✓ Divide your description into sections, such as bedroom, bathroom, living room, outdoor area, amenities, and extra services. For example:

    - Kitchen: Equipped with appliances and tools for eating and cooking like tables, chairs, refrigerator, kettle, bread toaster, microwave oven, and stove.

    - Living Room: A great space for bonding. It has a large sofa, three Chesterfield chairs, a 24 inch flat screen TV, and good lighting.

- Master Bedroom: Elegant with modern interior. This can accommodate three people with queen size bed, dresser, TV, and a closet. It has a private bathroom and air conditioning.

- Bedroom 2: Clean and has a classic interior. This room has two twin beds with air conditioning.

✓ Be specific. For example, instead of saying "the cabin is surrounded with trees", say "this small, one bedroom cabin is nestled in a sea of mahogany and pine trees".

✓ Don't be afraid to incorporate a little bit of humor into your listing. Remember that beauty attracts the eye, but it's the personality that wins the heart.

✓ Share insider knowledge about your neighborhood. This will make your description a little bit interesting.

Use simple words. Keep your sentences short. This is not an essay writing contest. So, you don't have to use all those hifalutin words.

SEO Hack #14: Write Interesting Photo Captions

They say that a photo paints a thousand words. This is true. But, you should also include amazing captions such as:

- "Romantic love nest perfect for honeymooners."
- "This condo has a breathtaking view of the city skyline."
- "Boho chic kitchen that exudes fun and eclectic vibe."

If you're posting a photo of the bed, describe how comfortable it is and what kind of mattress you use. It's also a good idea to use present tense verbs like sleep, write, eat, or work. This will encourage your potential guests to take action.

SEO Hack #15: Include The Speed of Your WiFi in Your Listing Description

A lot of travelers want to stay connected with their loved ones even if they are a thousand miles away. This is why you should position the speed of your WiFi as a selling point.

Here are a few tools that you can use to test your WiFi speed:

- http://www.speedtest.net/
- https://fast.com/
- http://speedtest.googlefiber.net/

SEO Hack #16: Include A Photo of Unique Shapes and Interesting Items in Your Property

To capture the character of your listing, take photos of unique items in your rental space. It could be attractive bottles, sculptures, paintings, or lamps.

SEO Hack #17: Optimize Your Nightly Price

If you're still new, you won't get as many bookings because you don't have a lot of ratings. You can't take advantage of the "word of mouth" marketing yet. There's no social proof.

So, to build your reputation, it's best to temporarily lower your price to encourage bookings.

Look up other listings in your area and find out how much they are charging. Then, charge a little lower than everybody else. Don't worry. You can gradually increase your price over time as you build your reputation. You can also charge for a cleaning fee to make up for the reduced price.

SEO Hack #18: Ask Friends to Add Your Listing on Their Wishlist

One of the best ways to increase your visibility on the search engine results is to get other people to click on the "heart" or "wish button".

When your listing is "wishlisted" many times, Airbnb thinks that your property is in demand. So, the system would slowly place you on page 1 of the search results. You can't control as to who wishlists your property. But, you can ask for friends and family to "wishlist" your property to help you boost your listing.

You must also use a really interesting and attractive picture as your cover photo. Most people wishlists properties with really great photos.

SEO Hack #19: Make Sure That Your Photo Looks Good on Mobile Devices

After you post your photos, log in to Airbnb using your mobile device and see if your photo looks good on your phone or tablet. If not, consider using another photo. Take note that photos with landscape format looks better than portrait photos.

You can't leave it all to luck. If you want to get more bookings, you have to take action.

SEO Hack #20: Link your Airbnb Listing to Your Social Media Accounts

Create social media accounts for your listing and then link them with your Airbnb account.

Linking your Airbnb listing to your Twitter, Instagram, and Facebook accounts increases your online visibility. This also makes it easier for you to promote your Airbnb listing on these social networking platforms.

Create a story and post photos of your unit regularly. Make sure that you post engaging content like the history of your neighborhood or your journey as an Airbnb entrepreneur. Also, don't forget to interact with your followers and respond to their comments and messages.

SEO Hack #21: Get a Popular Blogger to Feature Your Property

One of the best ways to improve your online presence is to get an influential blogger to feature your property. You can send a few travel bloggers a message and ask them to feature you in exchange of one or two night stay in your unit.

You can also send photos of your properties to various design blogs.

SEO Hack #22: Work with Your Local Tourism Officers

Reach out to your local tourism officers and ask them if they can feature your listing in their websites.

Local tourism websites are considered as trusted resources for tourists. So, getting listed in these websites can increase your bookings and build your reputation.

Chapter Recap and Your Action Plan

To become a superhost, you must have a huge influx of bookings. So, you should make your listing more visible on Airbnb search results. This way, it's easier to find you.

Here's what you should do to boost your Airbnb listing and make it more visible:

1. Place your location, famous local events, or popular tourist spots in your title. For example, "1BR Spacious Flat w/bathroom near Eiffel" or "3BR Townhouse near Coachella".

2. Respond to inquiries as fast as you can. If you have a full-time job, you can schedule your response time in the morning and in the evening. But, if you're a full-time Airbnb host, it's best to check your messages every two hours.

3. Update your calendar on a weekly basis. Make sure that your amenities, rates, and availability are up to date.

4. Give great service so you'll get five star ratings.

5. Keep a one night minimum requirement. Also, increase your maximum night limit. But, if you're not planning to be a long-term Airbnb host, it's best to keep your maximum night limit to just one week.

6. Offer a monthly discount if you want to be a long-term Airbnb host.

7. Enable the "instant booking" feature.

8. Search the top earners in your area. Study their listing and try to copy their "keywords".

9. Make sure that you have an attractive cover photo that exudes the overall vibe of your city.

10. Use bullet points, arrows, sections, and plus signs. This makes your listing more "scannable".

11. When you're starting, keep your nightly price low. This will help build your reputation.

Check and see if your photos and description looks good on mobile devices and make adjustments if necessary.

Chapter 7 – Be a Superstar Host: Get Five Star Ratings and Get More Bookings

If you want to earn tons of money through Airbnb, you have to get consistently high ratings. Why? Well, most people would want to book well-rated properties.

But, remember that you are rated on seven areas, including:

- Overall experience – Did your guests enjoy their stay in your property?
- Cleanliness – Did your guests find your unit tidy and clean?
- Accuracy – How accurate is your listing? Are you honest about how your place looks like? Did the guests get the amenities in your listing?
- Communication – Did you respond to your guest's queries in a timely manner?
- Arrival – Is the check-in process smooth and hassle-free?
- Value – Does your guests feel that they got good value for their money?
- Location – Does your guests feel safe in your neighborhood?

Below are some tips and hacks that you can use to become a superstar host and get a five star rating.

Superstar Host Tip #1: Be Friendly and Make A Good First Impression

Respond to your guests' inquiry in a timely manner. Make sure that you download the Airbnb app on your phone so it's easier for you to respond to queries. But, timely response is just not enough to get five star ratings. To become an Airbnb superstar, you must respond to your guests in a friendly manner. Speak to your guests as if you are talking to your close friends.

After you get an inquiry, you can say something like:

"It's a pleasure to meet you, Chris! Thanks for your inquiry! I am excited to have you here and see the city. We are just a few steps away Tootsie's Orchid Lounge.

What brings you to Nashville? Do you have specific spots you want to visit?"

This will help you make a good first impression.

Superstar Host Tip #2: Create a Detailed Guidebook

You must ensure that your guests have a fun and hassle-free vacation. One way to do this is to create a detailed guidebook.

One of the best things about Airbnb is that it allows travelers to explore cities like a local. So, it's important that you provide your guests insider tips on how to get the best out of your city.

Here are a few tips that you can use to create a detailed guidebook:

1. Your guidebook should include the following:

   ✓ *Tourist attractions* – What are the best attractions in your area. You can include temples, landmarks, architectural gems, and other interesting sights.

   ✓ *Things to do* – What can the guests do in your area? Can they skate in the park? Can they do scuba diving? Can they visit museums and see cabaret shows?

   ✓ *Restaurants* – Provide your guests a wide variety of restaurants with different menus and price range. For example, if you live in Cincinnati, you can tell your guests to go to Gomez Salsa (107 East 12th Street) or Findlay Market (1801 Race Street) if they want tasty and affordable meals. They can also visit Jean-Robert's Table (713 Vine Street) if they're having a date night.

   ✓ *Nightlife* – When you're on vacation, you just want to cut loose. This is why you should list all the nightspots in the city. You want your guests to have fun and get the most out of their vacation.

   ✓ *Free things to do* – List all the best free things to do in your city. It could be a free city tour or a free museum. Your guests would definitely thank you for this.

   ✓ *Shopping areas* – If you're traveling, you want to buy something that you can bring back home. So, make sure to include the shopping areas in your guide. Don't forget to include the flea markets and other areas where your guests can find unique items.

   ✓ *Things to note* – Does your city has a curfew or strict laws on cigarettes or alcohol? If so, make sure to include that in your guide book.

2. *Include a map of your city.* Make sure that this map highlights the best spots and restaurants in the cities. If you are renting out a large property, it's also a good idea to include a map so your guests would know where the bathroom is or where the bedrooms are.

3. *Incorporate your house rules in your guide.* You can write the "do's" and "don'ts". You can also include the off-limits area. If you're living in a condominium or an apartment, include the building rules.

4. You can print your guide and leave it in your home or you can just send it to your guest via email 48 hours before the check in time.

5. Include a house manual that includes important information like where the remote is, where the extra sheets are, how to turn on the AC, and how to use the coffee machine.

6. *Curate special experiences for your guests.* Take time to get to know your guests. Are they traveling for pleasure or business? Are they honeymooners or digital nomads? This way, you can recommend specific activities that are interesting to your guests. You don't have to create a unique manual for each guest. You can just add small details.

7. Place your WiFi password on the first page of your guide/manual.

8. *Your guide has to be fun and playful.* It's not a thesis, so don't be afraid to incorporate graphics and pictures. It also doesn't hurt to use a little humor.

Creating a guide/house manual increases your credibility. It also increases your chances of getting a five star rating.

Superstar Host Tip #3: Hire a Cleaner

If you're a bit obsessive compulsive, you should probably clean your unit yourself. But, do you have the time? Do you have the energy?

Cleaning takes away your focus from your rental business. So, it's best to leave it to the professionals.

Hiring a professional cleaner can be a game changer. Yes, it costs a little bit of money, but it also increases your profits in the long run. You can hire an individual to do it or you can pay a cleaning agency. You can incorporate the cleaning cost to your price or you can charge your guests an extra fee.

Superstar Host Tip #4: Get to Know Your Guests and Give them What They Need

Don't be afraid to ask your guests questions to figure out what they need. You can say something like "I look forward to having you here in our city. Are you traveling for work or vacation"? If your guest is traveling for work, you can provide a desk or a couple of pens. You can leave some beach balls and other things to play with if your guests are traveling for leisure.

Let's say that your unit is in Bali. People who go to Bali are usually running away from their daily stress. They just want to sit on the beach, drive around the area, and surf. So, you may want to provide your guests with beach towels or the contact number of the motorcycle rental service. You may also want to provide a surf board.

Superstar Host Tip #5: Be Proactive

To prevent a bad review, you have to be proactive. You must fix problems as they arise. Remember that your guests travel halfway around the world so problems could arise. Flights could get delayed and keys could get lost. So, find a way to alleviate your guests' stresses and problems.

Empathize with your guests. Be prepared to get up when your guests get locked out at night. Stay calm when you're faced with challenging situations and always deliver great customer service.

Superstar Host Tip #6: Do Not Show Up Unannounced

When you're a rookie host, you're naturally eager to please. It's great to be friendly with your guests, but don't overdo it. Do not show up unannounced. It's creepy and you're making your guests feel like they don't have privacy.

If you want to visit your guests and meet them in person, send them a message and ask them if you can drop by.

Superstar Host Tip #7: Have Enough Set of Towels

Towels are a bit bulky, so it's no surprise that travelers no longer bring one. This is why you should have enough towels. You should provide at least two towels for each guest.

Also, make sure you have at least four sets of towel. This way, you don't have to wash towels right after checkout. You'll always have a clean set of towels for new guests.

Superstar Host Tips #8: Optimize Your Time

An average Airbnb listing earns $14,000 a year. That's not bad for something that you're doing on the side. But, you can't spend all your time answering your guests' queries. So, it's wise to find ways to increase your efficiency.

Write down all the answers to frequently asked questions, so you can just easily copy and paste. This will save you a lot of time.

Superstar Host Tip #9: Always Update Your Photos and Description

Remember that what worked now may not work in the future, so you must update your listing regularly. If you decided to renovate your property, update your photos so there are no surprises. Your photos must reflect the current condition of your property.

Superstar Host Tip #10: Experiment

After you post your listing, observe and see how people respond to your listing. If you're not getting a booking after a week, make a few changes in your listing. You could change your profile or cover photo. You can add your location in the title and see what happens. This way, you'll know what works and what doesn't.

Just keep experimenting until you find the "sweet spot".

Superstar Host Tip #11: Provide a Welcome Package

A welcome package makes your guests feel more at home and well, welcome. It makes them feel important and it makes you likeable as a host. It's also one of the easiest ways to impress them, too.

Here are some ideas that you can use in preparing your welcome package:

1. *Include seasonal items.* If your guests are visiting during Chinese New Year, you can include chocolate coins and other items that bring good luck. You can also include gingerbread or sugar canes if your guests are staying over during the Christmas season.

2. Add practical items like soap, shampoo, body scrub, toothpaste, and disposable toothbrush. Why? Well, a lot of travelers forget to pack these essential items.

3. Add something delectable. You can include a bag of chips or roasted nuts.

4. Buy the items in bulk and pack your welcome packages once a month. This will save you a lot of time and money.

5. Personalize each welcome package by placing the small, DIY tag containing the guest's name.

Superstar Host Tip #12: Use Airbnb When You Travel

Being an Airbnb guest makes you a better host because it helps you pick up a few awesome hosting tips. It also helps you understand your guests a little bit more. So, the next time you travel, choose an Airbnb unit over a hotel.

Remember that Airbnb can suspend your account if you are getting a lot of bad reviews. So, you must strive to become an exceptional superstar host.

Superstar Host Tip #13: The Wow Factor

To be successful in the short-term rental industry, you must go an extra mile for your guests. Below are tips that can help you do that.

Leave Some Baked Goods

Who doesn't like a chocolate chip cookie or a great muffin? Bake your way to your guests' heart. But, don't worry if you don't have baking skills, you can just buy a few muffins or bread from your favourite bakery.

Don't buy too many baked goods. You can just leave a small box of cookies, muffins, and croissants. You can also leave local delicacies. For example, you can give your guests empanada if you live in Barcelona. You can also leave a few slices of pecan pie if your unit is in Dallas.

Have a Mini Gym

Do you know that fitness is the new status symbol? So, if you want to attract guests who are willing to pay good money for your place, you may want to invest in a mini-gym. You don't have to spend a lot. You can just buy a manual treadmill, a stationary bike, or a kettlebell. You can also leave a few exercise DVDs.

Build a Private Art Gallery

To wow your guests, you have to adorn your unit with beautiful art gallery. Having captivating art around the house will make your guests feel important and at home. You don't have to spend a lot to do this. You can find really cheap artworks at your local home depot. You can also create your own artworks if you have the talent for it.

If you're only renting out one room, avoid displaying family photographs around the home as this may make your guest feel like an outsider. Just display photographs of nature or local sights.

Place One Conversational Piece in Your Property

A conversational piece will make your property stand out. It can be a lavish lamp, a sand art sculpture, a grandfather clock, or a glowing mirror. You can also place glow in the dark stars on the ceiling of your guest room. You can also place indoor plant to make your guests feel like they are closer to nature.

Make Sure That Your Guests Have Things to Do

No matter how beautiful your unit is, you'll have a few bad reviews if the guests have nothing else to do than just sit around. So, it's important to include amenities like board games, DVDs, or a deck of cards.

Chargers

A lot of travelers forget their chargers, so it may be a good idea leave an extra charger for your guests.

Go Above and Beyond for Your Guests

Leave your phone number on the table and encourage your guests to contact you. You can even offer to tour your guests around your city if you have the time. Also, write down the nearest fire station, laundry shop, and money changer.

Superstar Host Tip #14: Network With Other Hosts

Reach out to other hosts and network with them. You can learn so much from them. You can also collaborate with them. A lot of Airbnb hosts meet and later on, decide to work together as co-hosts.

Chapter Recap and Your Action Plan

If you want to maximize your Airbnb earnings, you must consistently get high ratings. To do this, you must do the following:

1. Be honest. Do not exaggerate your amenities. Also, make sure to update your photos regularly.

2. Outline your check in process using Google Sheets and share it to your guests. Keep this process as simple and as hassle free as possible.

3. Create a detailed guidebook to help your guests maximize their trip. Your guide book should include a "house manual" containing basic information like your contact number, the WiFi password, and where to find the extra linens. Your guide should also include tourist attractions, things to do, nightlife, restaurants, maps, and shopping areas. Make this guide as colourful and attractive as you can.

4. Hire a cleaner to maintain your property.

5. Be proactive. Respond quickly to simple complaints, so you won't end up having a bad review.

6. Write down all the answers to FAQs so you can simply copy and paste them.

7. Automate and outsource when you can. Don't be afraid to use an app or hire someone to do the work for you, especially if you are managing multiple properties.

8. Impress your guests by offering a welcome package. If you can afford it, you can also offer amenities like a basket of baked goods, mini gym, private art gallery, and chargers.

9. Go to Airbnb events so you can meet fellow hosts. You can also join Airbnb host forums to learn insider tips and get the best practices of other short-term rental entrepreneurs.

To earn a lot of money on Airbnb, you should strive to master the art of hosting and become a short term rental superstar.

Chapter 8 – Reacting to Feedback and Reviews

You should take your guests' feedback seriously whether they're negative or positive. Be gracious and grateful when you receive a great feedback. But, be humble when you receive a negative review. Don't get upset. Don't be too proud. Don't take it as a personal attack because it's really not.

When you get a bad review, don't respond when you're angry. Let your head cool for a while before you write a response. It's also a great idea to acknowledge it and sincerely apologize for any inconvenience you have cost.

When you get a rating of 1, 2, 3, or 4, send your guest a message and ask what you could have done to get a five star review. Maybe you could move the furniture around, store more toilet papers, or clean your unit more often.

Buy a notebook and use it to record all the feedback you receive from your guests. Also, write down ideas that you can use to improve your space.

When you're ready, read all the feedback and ideas and make home improvements. You can buy a better bed, replace your wall paper, or improve your living room lighting.

Remember that "I'm sorry" is not enough. You have to take action. You must address issues to prevent similar complaints in the future.

Encourage Feedback

When you're confident that the customer is satisfied with your unit and service, encourage him to give you a review. Airbnb usually sends an email asking the guest to leave a review. You can also send your guest a message that goes something like this:

Dear _____,

It was a pleasure hosting you! I hope that you had a great experience staying at my place. To help attract more guests, would you be kind enough to write a detailed review of my Airbnb unit.

Thank you and I hope to see and host you again soon. xo

Encouraging reviews (especially from those who are happy with your service) can improve your reputation.

What to Do to Prevent Negative Reviews

No matter how nice you are or how clean your place is, you'll still get bad reviews from time to time. Don't take them personally. You just have to do everything that you can to avoid negative reviews. Here are a few tips that you can use:

1. Be proactive. Stop problems before they happen. Wow your guests by asking them what they need.

2. <u>Get a suggestion box and encourage your customers to give you their feedback directly</u>. This can eliminate comments like "the toilet paper breaks easily" or "the wall paper is ugly".

3. Give your guest a raving review right away. This will encourage him to return the favor and give you great reviews, too.

Can You Delete Bad Reviews?

No, you can't, but you can respond to them. Be professional when responding to bad reviews. Thank the customer for the feedback, acknowledge it, and most of all, apologize when necessary. It's also best to reach out to the customer directly to apologize or explain your side. When you write a review, keep your future guests in mind. Write a response that's powerful enough to undo the damage that the bad review has caused. You can write something like:

"Hi! I appreciate your feedback. That would really help me improve my unit. Know that customer satisfaction is my top priority. I'm sorry for any inconvenience and I will use your feedback to improve my service."

Chapter Recap and Your Action Plan

A customer's review can make or break you. But, how do you get positive feedback and how to react to negative feedback? Well, here's a list of tips that you can use:

1. Be proactive. Solve problems before they even happen.

2. Create a suggestion box. This helps you prevent a bad review.

3. Give your guests a positive review right after they left. This encourages them to return the favour.

4. If you received a bad feedback, don't worry. It's not the end of the world. You can always offset that with a positive feedback.

5. You can't delete bad reviews, but you can respond to them. Don't be defensive or too apologetic. Just focus on how much you appreciate the feedback and how it can help you improve your service.

You can't please everybody. From time to time, you'll get a bad feedback and when you do, use it to become a better host.

Part III – Airbnb as a Business

Airbnb has become so big that it has become a breeding ground for serious rentrepreneurs. This part talks about Airbnb as a business. In this part of the book, you'll learn about to select the right location and how to finance your Airbnb business.

Chapter 9 – How to Select the Right Location for Your Airbnb Business

Airbnb used to be just a side hustle, something that allows people to earn extra money out of their unused spaces. But, nowadays, Airbnb has become a hub for serious short term rental entrepreneurs (or rentrepreneurs).

If you're planning to build a short term rental empire, you should take advantage of tools like AirDNA.

AirDNA is a market and data analysis tool that you can use to analyze the vacation home rental industry and become a successful rentrepreneur.

AirDNA has an investment exploring that allows you to examine the revenue potential of short term vacation rental location in the United States and other countries. It helps you find profitable vacation rental markets. You can create a free AirDNA account here:

https://www.airdna.co/vacation-rental-data?utm_campaign=iy&utm_source=leaddyno&utm_medium=affiliate#_l_iy

, but you have to pay a premium of $19.99 a month to access its reports and analytics.

Before you even think of investing on properties for Airbnb rentals, you have to follow these steps:

1. *Find a location where Airbnb is one hundred percent legal.*

Airbnb is not one hundred percent legal in many states in the world. In fact, big cities like New York and Paris has strict rules on Airbnb rentals. Paris has issued more than one million euros worth of fines in 2018 to hosts who broke the rules. The city of Paris even sued Airbnb for unregistered apartment listings.

So, if you want to maximize your earnings and get the most out of your investment, you have to choose areas with less restriction on short-term rentals.

2. Choose the perfect property that has good earning potential.

AirDNA has a built in tool that calculates the earning potential of properties, so you could easily calculate the return on investment.

Top 25 Earning 2 Bedroom Properties in Regions Selected Above

City		Property ID	Bedrooms	Listing Title	FT Airbnb Earning Potential
Galveston		6326205	2	Canals Toys Fish Beach Close Fish Light Golf ..	$47,041
		2793406	2	The Coastal View	$37,219
		318246	2	Quite Cozy Home - 1 Blk From Beach	$37,080
		1966460	2	Sand & Serenity 1 blk From Beaches	$31,332
		7565124	2	cute,comfortable and affordable!	$30,744
		5808902	2	SAND & SEA - STEWART BEACH	$30,503
		4669729	2	Sugar Shack on the Gulf, upper unit	$29,652
		7128391	2	Expansive Gulf/Beach Front View	$29,292

The top earner here is a great example of why Airbnb investing requires going beyond

Let's say that you are eyeing a two bedroom property that costs $85,000. Let's say that the earning potential of that property is $45,000 a year. This means that you could earn a profit of $140,000 in just 5 years!

3. You have to factor in tourist arrivals.

Remember that the short-term rental industry caters mainly to tourists. So, you have to factor in tourist arrivals before you make an investment decisions. No matter how big the earning potential of a property is, you won't earn a lot if only a few people are traveling to your location.

4. Make sure that you have a positive cash flow.

When you calculate the costs vis-a-vis the expenses, you have to make sure that you have a positive cash flow. This means that your monthly earnings must exceed your monthly costs. This means that if your mortgage, pool cleaning fees, and house cleaning fees amount to $1,400 a month, you have to earn at least $2,000 a month from your property to get a profit of $600.

5. You must choose a property that's located in a sought-after neighborhood.

Location is everything when it comes to real estate investment, so make sure that your property is in close proximity to the major tourist spots in your city. You must choose a property that's just a few steps away from shopping malls, landmarks, shopping districts, and even the beach. Also, pick a place that has easy access to public transportation.

If your location happens to be less favorable, you just have to make the best out of it. Maybe it's not near the downtown area, but you can highlight a fact that it's just a few steps away from a restaurant and a park. You can also make your property unique and amazing. For example, you can add a pool or an indoor mini gym to make your property more marvelous and amazing.

According to AirDNA and other property investment websites, you should invest in the following cities:

✓ Key West, Florida

This island city may not be as popular as Miami, but it is also becoming a hot tourist destination. It has a few tourist spots like the Earnest Hemingway home and the picturesque Mallory Square. This city is known for its mansion-like houses and beaches.

Some properties in Key West can earn up to $7,600 a month and it has an annual cash return of 5. 22%. It also has an occupancy rate of 66%.

✓ Santa Barbara, California

The real estate properties in Santa Barbara are extremely expensive. But, they're worth every penny. This city looks glorious during the summer time. It also has a string of museums and parks. It has a projected earning potential of $4,522 a month. It also has an occupancy rate of 50 percent.

✓ Brookhaven, Georgia

Brookhaven is a quaint and quiet city that has already become a popular destination among travelers in the past few years. The city has an air of mystery. And yet, there's something about it that's elegant and classy.

Brookhaven has an occupancy rate of 42 percent and has a potential earning capacity of $3,187 a month.

✓ Panama City, Florida

According to Forbes, this village has one of the highest ROI (return on investment) on real estate properties. So, if you're looking to earn big bucks, invest in this city.

✓ Napa, California

Napa is known for its beautiful wineries. It's becoming one of the hottest tourist spots in California. So, it's no surprise that it's included in the list of high ROI cities according to Forbes.

If you're looking to invest in foreign lands, you must consider Nicaragua. This picturesque South American country has a string of beach towns like San Juan del Sur. You can also consider other profitable places like Auckland (New Zealand), Bucharest, Romania, Serbia, and Montenegro. These areas are not saturated, so you won't have a lot of competition.

<u>*Chapter Recap and Your Action Plan*</u>

Not all locations are the same. Use a data analytics tool like AirDNA to find the best places to invest in. You should also consider other factors (such as price, earning potential, and occupancy rate) before you invest in a property.

Chapter 10 – Automate Your Airbnb Account and Outsource Services

When you're just managing one listing, you feel like you can do everything. And you're right. But, if you have ten bookings a month or you're managing multiple listings, it's best to automate and outsource whenever you can.

Automate Your Responses and Manage Your Multiple Short Term Rental Accounts

IGMS is a vacation rental system that you can use to automate your Airbnb business and save a lot of time. It is currently managing 19,850 listings in 49 countries.

This service is free if you have four listings or less. It comes with single inbox, but you can use it to manage multiple Airbnb accounts and multiple calendars. It automates reviews. This means that right after your guests check out, they automatically get a five star review. This prompts them to write you a good review, too.

But, if you have 4 to 49 listings, this service can cost you $20 a month. It can cost you $30 (and a one-time set up fee of $2,500) if you have more than 50 listings. This package is perfect for property managers who oversee hundreds of listings around the world. It comes with a dedicated support specialist, a dedicated phone line, and branded emails.

We have reached out to IGMS, if you sign up using the below link you are eligible to receive 30% off on monthly subscriptions

https://www.igms.com/RickWong/30-bonus?afmc=5j

IGMS has a lot of awesome features, such as multi-platform synchronization, in-calendar rate charges, multiple account management, email templates, team management, parent & child bookings, and work orders.

Using automation tools like IGMS can benefit you in many ways, including:

1. It allows you to manage all your Airbnb accounts in one platform. So, you don't have to log in and out of your accounts one by one. This saves you a lot of time and increases your productivity, too.

2. Most automation tools have a multi-calendar feature. This is useful if you also listed your properties in other vacation rental sites like Clickstay, Booking.com,

Perfect Places, TheHolidayLet, Trips, and Tourist-Paradise. This feature makes sure that your properties don't get double-booked in different short term rental platforms.

3. It allows you to set up automated personalized replies. This increases your response rate and customer satisfaction. This also saves you a lot of time, too. IGMS also has an automated response system that reacts to triggers. You could program this system to send messages during "check in" or "check out". You can customize these messages. The automated response feature keeps you one step ahead of your competitors.

4. Automation tools allow you to add note to reservations like special instructions or requests.

5. It allows your cleaning staff to view their daily schedules and coordinate on "work orders" or special tasks.

6. It allows you to manage your team. This feature is especially useful if you are running a large short-term rental company.

Aside from IGMS, there are a lot of other automation tools that you can use, such as Superhost Tools, and Guesty.

Hire an Airbnb Cleaning Company

Remember that cleanliness is the key to getting a five star review. So, if you're managing multiple listings, it's best to hire a cleaning company. You can also hire a laundry and dry cleaning company to keep your sheets and towels clean.

There are a number of Airbnb cleaning companies that you can outsource, including:

- ✓ Maid This
- ✓ Tidy
- ✓ Turn Over BNB
- ✓ Maid Easy

You can also check yellow pages and find a reliable local cleaning company.

Automate Your Lights

Some guests do not bother to turn off the lights when they're not using it. This could shoot up your electricity bill. So, it may be wise to invest in a smart lighting system like Plum. This allows you to control your light switch remotely.

Consider Hiring A Property Manager

If you don't want to worry a thing about your Airbnb listing, it would be smart to consult a property management company.

Hiring a property management company has a lot of benefits. It can lower your costs and increase your revenue. Remember that property managers are professionals, using professional marketing and pricing strategies. This could help you maximize your income.

There are many property management companies that you can choose from in North America, such as:

- Evolve Vacation Rental – This is the top property management company in North America.
- Vacasa - This is based in Portland, Oregon and it operates in 17 states in the US.
- Senstay – This property management company operates in the Hamptons, Denver, Malibu, Palm Springs, and Scottsdale.
- Turn Key – This company manages over 2000 properties.
- Oasis Collections – This operates in five countries, namely Italy, Colombia, USA, Spain, and Brazil.
- Pillow – This company operates in different cities in California.

If you're not from North America, you have to consult a local property management company. There are a number of property management companies around the world.

Automation helps you manage your time well. It gives you more flexibility and it increases your earning potential. And most of all, it allows you to focus on things that you enjoy.

Chapter Recap and Your Action Plan

Automation increases your efficiency. It saves you a lot of time, too. So, don't be afraid to use automation tools, such as IGMS.

Chapter 11 – The Magic of "Self-Check In"

You don't want Airbnb to disrupt your life, so it's important to create an efficient self-check-in process. This means that your guests can automatically check in without your assistance. This saves you a lot of time and it's also less stressful to your guests. This process is also a kind of treasure hunt. It's a fun experience for your guests.

Here's how you can do it:

- ✓ Go to "Your Listings" and select a listing.
- ✓ Click on edit next to "Guest Resources".
- ✓ Click on "Add self check-in".
- ✓ Then, add your check in instructions.

To do this, you must have a lockbox with a combination key. Give the combination key. You can give the code to your guests a day before their check in time. You can also leave the key with your building receptionist/concierge if you have one.

To avoid confusion and complaints, you have to create a detailed instruction using Google Sheets. Be specific. Say something like "the lockbox is located at the left side of the main door, next to the mermaid statue". Once you're done, click on the "share" button and then, enter your guest's email add. Make sure you notify your guests that you have already shared the check in instructions.

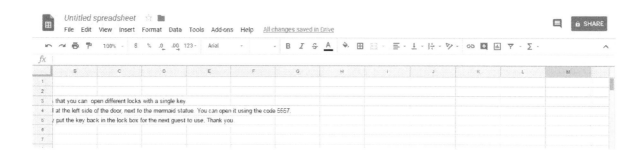

Also, it may be a good idea to provide one key that opens all doors in your house. This will save your guests from a lot of confusion and trouble. You can find a lot of master locks (multiple locks with one key) on Amazon. But, make sure that the bedrooms can be locked from the inside so your guests would feel safe.

Ask your guests to send you a message after they check in and check out. Why? Well, you won't know if you don't ask. Airbnb doesn't have a way of knowing if the guest actually checked in or not.

Why You Should Invest in Smart Locks

Key exchange can be a complicated process. This is the reason why you should invest in smart locks. It's convenient and secure. It also easily connects to security alarms, smart phones, and video surveillance cameras.

Smart lock systems usually have a home automation system that helps you become more aware of suspicious events in your property. Lastly, it's convenient. You don't have to hand a key to your guests. You can just give the code. It's a great investment. There are a lot of amazing smart lock brands in the market today, including August Smart Lock, Schlage Sense, Nest X Yale Lock, and Lockly Secure Plus.

Chapter Recap and Your Action Plan

Create a simple and clear "check in and check out" process using Google sheets and share it with your guests a few days before check in.

Also, invest in Smart Lock. This will make your check in process a lot easier.

Chapter 12 – Bookkeeping Tips to Manage Your Costs

It's not enough to have hundreds of bookings a year. To earn good money from Airbnb, you must learn to manage your costs as well. This is the reason why you should take bookkeeping seriously.

Bookkeeping helps you ensure that your Airbnb business has a positive cash flow. It also helps you make sound business decisions. It also reduces risks.

Here's a list of bookkeeping tips that you can use to turn your listing into a profit-generating machine:

1. Open a special checking account for your Airbnb business. This will make it easier for you to track your expenses and revenues. Remember that the things that you offer for free (soap, shampoo) are expenses. So, you have to be careful.

2. Get a dedicated credit card for your Airbnb business. This also makes it easier for you to track your Airbnb-related expenses. Keep your personal finances separate.

3. Keep records of all your expenses. Also, log your mileage when you use your personal car for business. This will help you maximize tax deductions.

4. Seek the service of a CPA, so you can get expert advice and service. A CPA can also do strategic tax planning, which can significantly reduce your tax payments. This will also give you an idea if your business is generating profit or expenses.

5. Use accounting software to track your revenues and expenses. You can use online accounting tools, such as Quickbooks, Zero, and Mint. You can also use Microsoft Excel, but make sure to categorize expenses. For example:

EXPENSES FOR JANUARY	
Utilities	
Item	**Amount**
Electricity	
Cable	
Internet	
Phone	
Gas	
Others	
Subtotal	
Mortgage	
Monthly Payment	

Subtotal	
Other Expenses	
Soap	
Toilet Paper	
Welcome Basket	
Shampoo	
Subtotal	
Labor	
Cleaning Services	
Landscaper	
CPA	
Subtotal	
TOTAL	

6. Review your bookkeeping data regularly.

You can do it twice a month or you can do it weekly if you have a lot of time. This will help you be on top of your finances.

Chapter Recap and Your Action Plan

At the end of the day, it's a business so you have to make sure that it's profitable. Meet with your CPA to get expert advice. You should also keep receipts of everything, so you can use them to maximize tax deductions.

Use an accounting software or app to track your expenses and revenue. This will help you maintain a positive cash flow.

Chapter 13 – Protect Yourself and Your Property

Airbnb operates in a "trust economy", but things aren't always plain sailing on Airbnb. You'd probably encounter destructive guests. You may also encounter creepy guests at some point, so you should protect yourself and your property.

Below are the tips that you can use to safeguard yourself and your property:

1. Get to know your guests before approving their booking request.

Ask your potential guests for their personal details, picture, phone number, credit card information, social media addresses, or government IDs. This may take a lot of work than usual, but it's always better to be safe than sorry.

2. Ask the neighbors to keep an eye of your property.

A growing number of people are using Airbnb for illegal activities such as prostitution, so ask someone to keep an eye on your property.

Airbnb provides protection, but this insurance does not include cash, shared areas, and pets.

3. Set clear house rules.

Be as clear and detailed and specific as possible. Don't leave a room for misinterpretation. For example, instead of saying "pets are not allowed", say "all types of pets are not allowed". Instead of saying "illegal activities are not allowed", you can say "any illegal activity is prohibited, including prostitution and use of illegal drugs".

Remember that if a guest does not follow your house rules, you can cancel the reservation immediately without penalty.

4. Be a friendly and accommodating host.

It's important to be accommodating and to maintain an open communication line with your guests. Why? Well, if you're friendly, your guests are more likely to respect your property. Who knows? You may earn new friends, too.

5. Make sure that your property is insured.

In theory, Airbnb has an airtight insurance that protects its hosts. But, in reality, it's pretty hard to file a claim. A lot of hosts are happy with the compensation they got from the host protection program. But, a lot of hosts also claimed that their claim/problem was not resolved.

To be safe, make sure that you have all the insurance you need.

Chapter Recap and Your Action Plan

It's better to be safe than sorry. So, make sure that you have a clear house rules that leave no room for misinterpretation. You should also make sure that your property is insured and ask your neighbors to keep an eye on your property.

Conclusion

I'd like to thank you and congratulate you for transiting my lines from start to finish. I hope that this book can help you become a superhost, maximize your Airbnb earnings, and achieve financial freedom.

Now, let's review the major points of this book:

- ✓ Airbnb is an online marketplace that you can use to rent out your property and earn extra money. You can even use it as a tool in building your short term rental empire.

- ✓ Before you list your property on Airbnb, you should check your local laws. A lot of cities prohibit short-term rentals. You must also check with your landlord so you won't have problems later on.

- ✓ Upgrade and renovate your home if you need to.

- ✓ Check if you are built for hosting. You see, not everyone can be a great host. You must be passionate about property management. You must also have great customer service skills.

- ✓ Airbnb has a Host Protection Program that covers property damage and lawsuits. But, you must know that this insurance program does not cover everything. It does not cover lost jewelry, artwork, heirlooms, and collectibles. It's still best to get your own insurance.

- ✓ You must consider the following factors in setting your nightly price – property tax, mortgage payment, cleaning service fee, maintenance fee, and Airbnb fees.

- ✓ You must be clear about your goals. How much do you want to earn from Airbnb? What type of host do you want to become? Do you just want to earn extra money or do you want to be a successful rentrepreneur?

- ✓ Your Airbnb earnings depend on a lot of factors like your location, the nature of your property, the size of your unit, and the amount of your competition. To earn more money, you may want to consider managing multiple properties.

- ✓ Post photos that showcase the beauty of your unit. Use natural lighting as much as possible. Also, take photos in landscape format. This maximizes the space and it also looks good on mobile devices.

- ✓ To maximize your Airbnb earnings, strive to be a superhost. Being a superhost comes with a number of cool benefits. It increases your credibility and earnings.

- ✓ Schedule your Airbnb time, so you can respond to all your messages within 24 hours.

- ✓ Be honest to your guests. Do not exaggerate your amenities or oversell your property.

- ✓ To increase your popularity as a host, you must go an extra mile for your guests.

- ✓ Include your location in your listing title. This will make it easier for guests to find your property on Airbnb. You can also include popular events in your title.

- ✓ Your listing description should be scannable.

- ✓ Use simple, but descriptive words when you're writing your description. Use words that speak to your target audience.

- ✓ Highlight your unique selling point.

- ✓ A superhost is an experienced host that consistently delivers exceptional service to guests.

- ✓ Superhosts usually get priority support. Their listings are also visible to a wider audience and they usually get invited to the most exclusive Airbnb events.

- ✓ You must have 50 percent review rate to become a superhost.

- ✓ If you have a "day job", schedule your Airbnb response time twice daily – 40 minutes in the morning and another 40 minutes in the afternoon.

- ✓ Verify your offline ID to increase your credibility and trustworthiness.

- ✓ Respond to guest inquiries as fast as you can.

- ✓ Update your calendar regularly.

- ✓ Set your price low, especially when you are still starting.

- ✓ Most Airbnb user decisions are made based on photos. So, you have to make sure that your photos are attractive, eye catching, and interesting.

- ✓ Link your listing to your Facebook, Instagram, and Twitter accounts.

- ✓ To improve the overall experience of your guests, it's a good idea to create a guidebook that includes tourist attractions, restaurants, nightlife, and shopping areas.

- ✓ Hire a cleaner.

- ✓ To carve your name in the short-term rental industry, you must wow your guests.

- ✓ Build a relationship with fellow hosts. This will help you learn a number of insider tips that can help you become a better host.

- ✓ To increase your revenue, you must consider managing multiple listings.

- ✓ Place a suggestion box in your property. This will significantly reduce your complaints and bad ratings.

- ✓ No matter how good you are as a host, you will get bad reviews and difficult guests from time to time. When this happens, you must learn to take criticisms graciously.

I hope that these tips and strategies are able to help you establish yourself as a reliable, trustworthy, and successful Airbnb host.

I wish you the best of luck!

We hoped you enjoyed this book!

As small publishing business, we at Entrepreneurial Pursuits, are operated by the everyday folk, our editor is a stay at home single mom with two kids in Wisconsin, while our designer is a recently laid off worker.

It would really help our small business if you can give us an honest review of our book **here**

Thank you!

Made in the USA
Las Vegas, NV
10 December 2021

36888764R00065